# BEING THE MESSAGE

# BEING
# THE MESSAGE

## LESSONS LEARNED ON THE
## FRONTLINE OF MISSION

ANDY **HAWTHORNE**
AND FRIENDS

First published in Great Britain in 2017 by The Message Trust
Lancaster House, Harper Road
Manchester, M22 4RG, UK

Reprinted 2018.

ISBN 978-1-9999036-0-2
eISBN 978-1-9999036-1-9

Editor: Alistair Metcalfe
Cover design and typesetting: Simon Baker
Photography: Hannah Beatrice Owens

*For The Message team – mates on a mission to see lives transformed by Jesus Christ*

# Contents

# Foreword

## SIR BRIAN SOUTER, CHAIRMAN, STAGECOACH GROUP

It's an honour to be asked to write a brief foreword to this wonderful new book from Andy, Carl and the Message team.

Like them, I know what it's like to grow an organisation from the ground up – in our case from a couple of second-hand buses to a global transport company, Stagecoach Group, and an investment business, Souter Holdings.

We too have learned plenty of lessons along the way – and I'm glad to say that one of them is that charitable giving should be embedded in the business philosophy of our companies.

Recently I heard the Filipino Cardinal Luis Tagle say, 'People are told that money cannot bring happiness, but that's not true. Money can bring happiness – if you give it away.'

We wholeheartedly agree. It's quite simply one of the greatest sources of happiness in the world, to give generously. And it's especially true when you find a partner who shares your values and your heart.

My wife Betty and I have supported The Message for over a decade now, quite simply because we believe in the message of The Message Trust.

For me, Christianity gives us the three things human beings most need. First of all, it gives us a set of rules to live by. Listen to the stories of transformation from The Message's work, and you quickly realise that one of the biggest problems we have in our society is that young people need guidance to live wisely. I was one of them: I think I spent more time in the corridor than I did in the classroom at school!

The truth is, though, that rules in themselves are not enough – we also need role models. As I've heard the stories of young people reached in schools, Eden communities and prisons, the one thing you hear more than any other is 'I didn't have a good role model growing up.' But in the man Christ Jesus, we have the best role model there is. That's why The Message's work points to Jesus as the One sent from God to love the last, the least and the lost.

But for me, Christianity is about more than both rules and role models, as important as they are. For in Jesus Christ I have found a Redeemer. I need Jesus because he's the only person who has the power to forgive my sins, to change my life and to give me purpose and direction. It is a power greater than I can find anywhere else in the world. That power of the presence of Jesus Christ is absolutely at the centre of The Message Trust's message.

What this brilliant little book shows is that this power is also at the heart of The Message's culture. It is deeply embedded in the way they work. They know they depend daily on the favour of God, and they will do whatever it takes to attract it.

It's no mean feat to build an organisation that attracts people to sacrificially lay down their lives on Eden estates and in prisons, that inspires talented performers to give up careers in the music industry to share the gospel in schools, that inspires people like me to give financially – and most importantly, that sees thousands of young people's lives transformed every year as a result.

Read on and learn how what The Message team has discovered might help you, your church or your organisation know the favour of God and bring the hope of Jesus Christ to the world around you.

*Sir Brian Souter, Edinburgh, 2017*

# Introduction

**ANDY HAWTHORNE OBE**

Does culture really 'eat strategy for breakfast'?

At the beginning of 2017 we were thrilled to find out that The Message Trust had been rated one of the top 100 charities to work for in the UK. As such, my wife Michele and I were invited along to the Sunday Times UK Charity Awards at a glittering dinner in London. We were surrounded by the good and the great of the non-profit sector – leaders of charities like UNICEF, the Royal National Institute for the Blind, The Salvation Army, and many others. We went along with little expectation of any particular success, and were just glad to enjoy the champagne and fancy food.

After the dinner, the Awards ceremony began, and TV presenter Ben Shephard ran down the top 100 list in reverse order, ranked according to the Sunday Times' own research. As the evening went on, my mouth fell further and further open – until The Message

Trust was announced as the runner-up! We were officially named the second best Not-For-Profit Organisation to work for in the UK. To top it all, I was personally awarded the trophy for the Top UK Charity CEO. I was gobsmacked.

As I made my way up to the podium, I felt genuinely humbled, wondering at how this guy with nothing more than one O-Level and a lot of passion had managed to beat all these high-flying and brilliant charity executives with their MBAs. I knew the answer then, and am still convinced now, that it's called the favour of God. The Lord really has been on this thing called The Message, as, over 25 years, we have gone from a one-man-band to a global movement that is touching the lives of literally hundreds of thousands of young people, often from the most broken of backgrounds.

The awards also gave me a bit of confidence to recognise that we have something very special here at The Message, and a desire began to grow in me to share some of the things we have learned and put in place that we believe have led to God so graciously blessing what we have tried to do for him. The difference between trying to do something in your own strength and something that attracts the Lord's favour is the difference between chalk and cheese. I feel if we can share some stuff that will help others build their own lives and organisations well, then that's a job well done.

In the business world, there is a lot of talk about culture being super-important. Louis V. Gerstner, the CEO of IBM, once claimed, 'Culture is everything,' and Mark Fields, President of the Ford Motor Company famously said, 'Culture eats strategy for breakfast.' This is surely true. But it's only one of three particular things which

I think a kingdom business or charity leader needs to give prayerful attention to.

The Message Trust started 25 years ago but the work of The Message was actually birthed 30 years ago out of a business I owned with my brother, Simon. It was the messy lives of some of the young men we employed in inner-city Manchester that prompted us to organise an outreach event called Message '88, climaxing, after hundreds of local events for young people, in a week at the Apollo Theatre which was then Manchester's largest and most prestigious rock venue.

The night Simon and I first had the idea for what would become, as far as I know, Manchester's largest ever youth outreach, I went home buzzing, and full of faith. But it wasn't long before all sorts of doubts, fears and legitimate questions came to mind such as: 'Who do you think you are?', 'You haven't got the resources, the gifting or the connections to pull this off!' and 'Forget it right away!' It's times like this that the best thing you can do is pray, read your Bible and check in with some other Christians to see what they think.

So I prayed and opened my Bible and thank God, my set reading for the day was Isaiah 43:18-21, scriptures you will now find all over our headquarters, verses that in some ways we have never left in the following 30 years:

'Forget the former things; do not dwell on the past. See, I am doing a new thing! Now it springs up; do you not perceive it? I am making a way in the wilderness and streams in the wasteland. The wild animals honour me, the jackals and the owls, because I provide water in the wilderness and streams in the wasteland to give drink to my people, my chosen, the people I formed for myself that they may proclaim my praise.'

The reason I love these verses so much is because they speak of everything I want The Message to be about.

Firstly, *God-given strategy*. God is doing a new thing all over the world to see the Great Commandment to love God and love our fellow man, and the Great Commission to make him known and make disciples, happen. Our goal is to perceive this strategy and to fulfil our bit of it. That's why prayer and seeking his will is absolutely foundational to us at The Message and, as the founder and CEO, I see it as my personal responsibility to test the prayer temperature and make sure prayer happens and stays hot every day as we grow this work. God's Word sets the direction and the strategy is born in prayer.

My experience is that once you've got the strategy from the Lord, *then he starts to bring the people* along in a remarkable way to fulfil it. Often, they're not the ones you might expect him to bring along. Some of our very best leaders are people who before they met Christ could fairly be described as 'wild animals' but who have now gone from being the problem to the answer and are now living lives that honour him. Is there anything more beautiful than that? I am surrounded by people, some of whom have helped to write this book, who actually make me look good. People who are far more intelligent, talented and qualified than me, who have been similarly gripped by a God-given strategy to make a mark in this generation through The Message.

Once you've got a great strategy and some great people who have well and truly bought into it, then you've got a chance of developing that *all-important culture to underpin it all*. Without people who are on-side with your vision and values, you can work as hard as you like to develop a world-class culture, but it ain't gonna happen!

I spend a lot of my time visiting other organisations – charities, businesses and churches – and it is fair to say you can pretty much sniff the culture of a place, for good or ill, within about five minutes of walking in the door. I know we are not perfect, and I'm determined we don't rest on our laurels, but I am super proud of our culture at The Message.

I reckon it's our responsibility as leaders to constantly monitor and do all we can to cultivate the right kind of culture. Much of this is done through celebrating any time we see the kind of prayerful, sacrificial, gracious, fun-loving, passionate culture we want. I guess I want to be a bit like one of those sniffer dogs you often see at the airport – when they get a sniff of what they are looking for, they are trained to go crazy. When I get a sniff of the right kind of culture, I need to find multiple ways of barking at the top of my voice and wagging my tail wildly!

That's the heart behind this book – an attempt to capture what it is that we think makes The Message who we are, in our own words. Second Chronicles 16:9 says 'For the eyes of the Lord range throughout the earth to strengthen those whose hearts are fully committed to him.' We know we don't have everything down, but we believe in some key ways our heart and our habits have attracted the favour of God over these last 25 years. So I believe there's something in here for everyone to learn – whether you lead a charity, a business or a church, or you're just seeking to know the favour of the Lord in your own life, work and relationships with others.

I'm excited that it's not just my voice throughout these chapters but the voices of a whole team who have been pulling together for years. There is distilled wisdom here about mission and prayer, serving the poor, sacrificial generosity, wholehearted discipleship and leading with courage. If something about one chapter doesn't resonate with you, keep reading – there's sure to be something that speaks to you in the next one.

A little while ago, something happened that really brought joy to my heart. We were showing some senior people around from the local council who, as far as I know, weren't Christians. At the end of their tour they said, 'Wow, it's amazing here – it's like Google!' I think I know what they meant – it's a creative, up for it, dynamic culture where the team are all pulling in the same direction.

More and more let that be so, as we feed on the dynamic breakfast, lunch and dinner of great God-given strategy, the beautiful gifted-ness of people, and a passionate culture.

# CHAPTER 1

# Keep Mission Hot

## CARL BEECH, DEPUTY CEO

*'The shortest and surest cut to civilisation is salvation' – William Booth*

I am an evangelist. Since the day I first met Christ on April 22, 1990 at around 7pm, I knew that I would be devoting the rest of my life to telling people about him. How could I not do that? The sheer realisation of what I had been rescued from, and rescued for, was simply mind-blowing. From that moment on, I knew evangelism would be the sole cause of my life. I've worked it out in many different ways since then: by sharing my faith in the bank where I worked, by planting churches, and by leading evangelistic organisations. But it's always been about mission.

Now, as a deeply committed part of the Message movement, I often find myself deeply buried in management accounts, fundraising for our ministry, making strategic decisions, speaking at various events and churches, writing and broadcasting, and leading a talented team of senior leaders. And still, all of it has the single aim of communicating the message of Jesus as widely as we can, and giving our teams their best 'shot at goal' in doing so. I see my role as to keep mission front-and-centre, and to ensure that all we do focuses on that one crucial goal.

For years now we have seen in our nation a gradual and creeping coldness to the gospel of Jesus. As a result, many of us at the coalface have tried to find creative and practical ways of communicating the love of God, because we felt that people's ears were completely closed to the gospel message. Of course, compassion and love for people, which flows from a love for God, is critical – and certainly not misplaced! You can't be an evangelist if you don't love people. And so back in the day, my friends and I tried everything we could to build bridges with people.

In my case, that was particularly with the poor and marginalised. This stemmed in part from a weird experience I had as a kid, travelling up on the London Underground to see my Dad at his work. I was only about five years old, but I can vividly remember sitting on the train, travelling past all the bust-up and dilapidated blocks of flats and wastelands of the East End of 1970s London, and feeling a deep sadness about it. I can even remember saying to my Mum that I didn't like it, and that one day, I was going to change it! I believe, looking back, that this was one of the first moments God started to place his call on my life to serve him, even though I didn't grow up in a church-going Christian home.

Fast forward to 1996, and I had just left my career in banking to train to be a Baptist minister on a church planting course at Spurgeon's College. The course was structured so that I could attend college for two days a week for three years, while planting a church at the same time. To cut a long story short, my wife Karen and I decided to plant on an estate in Essex that in some ways was extremely broken. Why? Partly because I couldn't shake off God's heart for the poor.

Listen to these amazing words from Isaiah 58:6-14…

> "'Is not this the kind of fasting I have chosen: to loose the chains of injustice and untie the cords of the yoke, to set the oppressed free and break every yoke? Is it not to share your food with the hungry and to provide the poor wanderer with shelter – when you see the naked, to clothe them, and not to turn away from your own flesh and blood? Then your light will break forth like the dawn, and your healing will quickly appear; then your righteousness will go before you, and the glory of the Lord will be your rear guard. Then you will call, and the Lord will answer; you will cry for help, and he will say: Here am I.

> "If you do away with the yoke of oppression, with the pointing finger and malicious talk, and if you spend yourselves in behalf of the hungry and satisfy the needs of the oppressed, then your light will rise in the darkness, and your night will become like the noonday. The Lord will guide you always; he will satisfy your needs in a sun-scorched land and will strengthen your frame. You will be like a well-watered garden, like a spring whose waters never fail. Your people will rebuild the ancient ruins and will raise up the age-old foundations; you will

be called Repairer of Broken Walls, Restorer of Streets with Dwellings.

"If you keep your feet from breaking the Sabbath and from doing as you please on my holy day, if you call the Sabbath a delight and the Lord's holy day honourable, and if you honour it by not going your own way and not doing as you please or speaking idle words, then you will find your joy in the Lord, and I will cause you to ride in triumph on the heights of the land and to feast on the inheritance of your father Jacob." For the mouth of the Lord has spoken.'

Or these, from Luke 4:18...

'The Spirit of the Lord is on me, because he has anointed me to proclaim good news to the poor. He has sent me to proclaim freedom for the prisoners and recovery of sight for the blind, to set the oppressed free.'

## WHAT'S MISSING?

So, in complete naivety and with no training or salary to back us up, we went for it. We poured our hearts into that little estate. And nothing happened – I mean *nothing*! We tried desperately to build bridges with people. We did all that we could to meet the needs of the poor. We had a furniture bank and gave out free food before food banks were even a thing. We visited people, cleaned up their gardens, tidied houses, sat with the lonely, and befriended perpetrators of domestic violence, addicts, and people struggling with debt. We helped people make temporary gains, only to see them slip back again into their old ways. It was tough and heart-breaking. After 18 months of tireless and emotionally draining work, we literally had very little to show for our efforts. Certainly no long-term change.

We had built loads of relationships, we knew lots of people, we had tried to meet many needs – but the church was empty. Why? Because no one had come to Christ and surrendered their lives to him. Why? After some tough analysis and soul-searching, we realised that we simply hadn't been telling people about Jesus properly or been inviting people to follow Him.

We made some changes and the outcomes were, well, spectacular! Within 18 months of this gospel epiphany we had households of Christians on nearly every road of our estate. Not only that, but the changes in the community were staggering, including the local police remarking to me that they were being called to the estate less.

Only the gospel of Jesus Christ makes permanent and lasting change. I've carried this truth with me for the last 20-plus years, and for us at The Message it is a deeply held conviction. We have a special heart for young people and the poor but we are of the deep conviction that only the gospel can bring lasting and eternal transformation of people's lives. Every week at The Message, we hear new stories that underscore our conviction that we must 'Keep Mission Hot.'

One area of our work is in prisons. Our teams go into prisons every week, running Alpha courses, group workshops, taking chapel services and generally communicating Jesus to people. When ex-offenders come out of prison, we have houses and businesses to give those we have been working with a shot at a job, training and a home to live in. It really is beautiful work and when I first came across the Message Enterprise Centre, I truly thought this was a little glimpse of heaven on earth. I knew deep in my soul that it was pleasing to God. If you ask me, the results also speak of God's pleasure. Come through a government ex-offenders' programme and the likelihood is that around 80% of the time you will reoffend. Come through The Message Trust's programme and the likelihood that you will reoffend drops to under 10%. That's astonishing, right? The reason is simple. We call it 'Christ-centred enterprise.' Jesus is right at the centre of all that we do, and our team members are in an atmosphere where the temperature is hot!

The same goes for our Eden teams. Eden is an incredible ministry of long-term missionaries who choose to be 'downwardly mobile' and live in the toughest estates and inner cities of the UK. I'll never forget hearing the story of one lady who had recently been baptised. Her life had been hell. Attacked by her partner (even having dogs set on her), suffering fear, intimidation and all kinds of personal trauma, she stood there glowing as she talked about how Jesus had totally transformed her life, given her self-esteem back, and brought peace and emotional healing. And it wasn't temporary – I bumped into her months later when preaching at a church many miles away from Message HQ and she came bounding over to me, absolutely full of life.

I'll say it again – only Jesus can bring this kind of transformation and I'm in awe of those in our movement who sacrificially invest their lives into communicating his message in dark and broken places. Why do they do it? Because they know the gospel works!

## RAISING THE TEMPERATURE

So, how do we keep mission hot? It's actually quite simple – we talk about Jesus. A lot! Every morning we gather to pray and hear teaching from the Bible. We especially study the things that Jesus said and did. We ensure that wherever we go on mission, two things are always done – first we communicate Christ clearly. And second, we invite people to commit themselves 100% to Jesus' mission. In many ways, that's our calling card.

We hold all our teams to account on the mission. Setting up new and innovative projects is something we do regularly, and well – but we insist that they always have the aim of communicating the gospel. We have world-class bands performing at schools, prisons, and gigs big and small all over the country. But wherever they go, they know they are there to communicate the gospel. When they come back they tell us the stories of transformation.

I have the privilege of hearing regular reports from teams all over the country – they share of how kids and adults have wept in the presence of God, of how when they have gone back they have met kids who stopped self-harming after meeting Jesus and how suicidal thoughts left them. We've seen young people encounter Jesus though Message teams, then join our Academy and go on to be leaders in the movement. Jesus Christ truly changes everything in a person's life.

We also invest into training a global network of men and women to be bold evangelists. One critical part of our movement is the Advance Evangelists' Network. Ben Jack explains more in Chapter 10. These are groups of new or established evangelists, who are committed to mentoring and equipping each other, meeting regularly, holding each other accountable and sharing best practice with the aim of sharpening each other up for full-on and effective gospel proclamation. Many of us are leading these groups as part of what we do with the aim of raising up hundreds of evangelists. It's a genuine joy to get emails every week from evangelists working all over the world with story after story of people committing their lives to Christ!

Telling the stories from across the movement is a key method of keeping mission hot. There's enough bad news out there to keep our heads down, but sharing gospel stories lifts them up like nothing else. At heart, we are gospel people and we know the message of the cross is what makes the difference. I will never forget the first time I had an email from a fledgling evangelist in my Advance group after I had coached him in how to communicate the gospel, and in particular how to invite people to respond in a bold, courageous and clear way. The following Sunday he told me how three people had committed their lives to Christ and that he had never seen that before from his preaching. Not only did I feel totally pumped, but it spurred me on to get out there and ask people to respond that night at an event where I was preaching – and they did! Come on! Stories build faith.

If you are passionate about the gospel, then I'm of the deep conviction that there is no better place to be than on the front line of evangelism. Whenever we recruit someone in a ministry position at The Message, we ensure that they are as passionate as we are to communicate Jesus. If they're not, they probably wouldn't fit in with us. If they are, they find themselves part of a crazy movement that truly believes that the gospel can change the world.

# CHAPTER 2

# Keep Prayer Hot

## ANDY HAWTHORNE, FOUNDER AND CEO

*God moves in response to our passionate, disciplined prayer*

I am sometimes asked if, as Founder and CEO, I have a job description at The Message. The answer I like to give is, 'Yes – and it only has two lines: "Keep Mission Hot, and Keep Prayer Hot!"' My job is, of course, a bit more complicated than that. But what I have discovered is that if I focus my efforts on those two things, everything else tends to look after itself.

'Keep Mission Hot, and Keep Prayer Hot', in my opinion, should actually be the job description of every Christian leader. Carl Beech explained in the last chapter what we do to keep mission central to everything we do at The Message. It's been a beautiful thing to have Carl with us over the last couple of years, helping to lead the charge towards those who don't know Jesus.

But all my experience shows that mission without prayer is pretty powerless. That's why we put equal amounts of focus and attention on keeping prayer hot, too. Practically, this involves various things such as our prayer room at the heart of our HQ in Manchester, where team members are encouraged to go to seek wisdom and revelation from the Lord. Every day starts with team prayer and every Tuesday there is a special extended prayer meeting that everyone is encouraged to drop into, between 12 and 3pm.

Perhaps most important of all are our Prayer Days. Once a month we all 'down tools' and give a whole day to prayer, worship, testimonies and inspiration. The decision to do this, and keep doing it, is probably the best one I ever made regarding the direction of The Message. I sometimes wonder if we would have made it this far without our Prayer Days – so often our breakthrough in terms of financial provision or new partnerships has come on the back of these extended times of prayer and worship. I have seen them grow from four or five people and an acoustic guitar to around 200 of the most awesome Jesus followers you could imagine and a full-on, amazing worship band leading us into God's presence.

## PRAYER WITH PASSION AND EXPECTATION

I've become convinced that there are actually two types of prayer – praying, and then praying in the Spirit. This is when you've broken through, the atmosphere is electric, and you just know God is hearing and answering your prayers. My experience is that often, this kind of praying in the Spirit takes time. Often I come to Prayer Days with a head full of distractions, and sometimes even a heart full of sin, and this can be a real hindrance. It needs dealing with if we are going to see the breakthroughs we long for.

Our Prayer Days embody the three things that I think city-changing, world-shaking prayer always involves:

**Faith.** In the atmosphere of faith that is engendered at these days as powerful testimonies are shared, it's easy to dream big and believe that God is going to do bigger stuff in the future. So much of what we experience as a team and individually is 'according to our faith' (Romans 12:3) and if the Bible says, 'anything is possible for the person who has faith' (Mark 9:23) but also 'it's impossible to please God without faith' (Hebrews 11:6), then obviously, faith is pretty important. The Message is a faith ministry from start to finish and if our Prayer Days help to stir up more faith in us and more faith-filled adventures on the back of them, then that's a result.

**Unity.** As far as I can see, there has never been a revival birthed without united sacrificial prayer and fuelled through passionate gospel preaching. I guess it's likely, therefore, that if God is ready to do something big in our nation, he will stir up people into the humility of prayer and fire them up into the foolishness of preaching. It's not just any old prayer that really shifts things, however, but *united* prayer, when God's people forgive their relatively small disagreements and divisions and get on with getting on together. At The Message, we often talk about being 'mates on a mission'. God is looking for mates who realise that too much is at stake for petty differences and minor offences to be allowed to take root. Our Prayer Days can be the place for people to deal with stuff without allowing the deadly disunity that stifles so many ministries and churches to grow. As we pray and passionately worship, so often God deals with the sticky stuff we bring to our Prayer Days and gets us all back on track.

**Holiness.** Our primary calling at The Message is as evangelists, and as such we love to do two things – tell people who don't know Jesus about Jesus and, if we can't do that, then to tell people who know Jesus to tell people who don't know Jesus about Jesus! That's good, but as evangelists we have watch over our lives carefully. If we are not genuinely rooted in fellowship and connected to a group of other believers, we can quickly become the kind of people who think it's smart to show a lost world how far Christians can go in terms of language, drinking, joke-telling or whatever, and seriously think that this kind of compromise is going to be attractive to people who aren't yet Christians. Truthfully, it's only the holiness of Jesus, lived out in real and relevant ways that will heal a broken world, not our attempts to ape the culture. That's why, as evangelists, we need to spend quality time praying and pressing into Jesus and allow the Holy Spirit to reveal to us any areas of our lives that are out of step, or even completely out of order. Again, Prayer Days, as the spiritual temperature hots up, are a perfect place for this to happen.

Anybody who has spent any time around The Message will know that the early days of the Salvation Army have been a huge inspiration to us. The Salvationists of William and Catherine Booth's era were utterly fearless and wildly creative. They loved the poor and the lost with a passion, often embracing great suffering, which are all good signs of a truly Jesus-centred ministry.

The thing that many who rejoice in the glory days of the Salvation Army are sometimes slow to realise, though, is just how much they loved holiness of heart and life. So-called 'holiness meetings' were held every week in Salvation Army missions around the world to help lead Christians, often from the most broken backgrounds imaginable, into that beautiful place of a sanctifying experience of Jesus. The Booths and their holy army had learnt that all the great mission plans and sacrificial prayer weren't going to get the job done unless they were backed up by a holy life.

## MUCH PRAYER EQUALS MUCH BLESSING

As a fairly new Christian, I was involved in taking coaches to the Billy Graham Mission England events in the North West. As a Manchester United fan, it was a bit of a struggle to invite my friends and family to Anfield, the home of Liverpool FC, but it was definitely worth it when I watched them get out of their seats and go onto the pitch to give their lives to Christ, as the great man brought the invitation.

In the build-up to Mission England, I went to an event at the Free Trade Hall in Manchester, and Billy Graham appeared by live link from the United States. The guy who interviewed him asked what the three key things were that we should be doing as the mission approached. Billy thought for a moment and then said, 'The first thing is definitely to pray. The second thing is to pray. And, in fact, the third thing is to pray!' Billy had learnt over decades of large mission events across the world that the success of an outreach is not primarily based on slick organisation or publicity, but on sacrificial prayer.

Much prayer really does equal much blessing, as surely as little prayer equals little blessing. I certainly know what I want for The Message and the things I'm involved in. As Leonard Ravenhill, the slightly scary but amazing revival preacher, once said, 'The Devil laughs at our work, mocks our labours, pours scorn on all our efforts, but trembles when we pray.'

Is it any wonder that I feel a massive responsibility to constantly test the prayer temperature at The Message, and to do all I can to keep prayer hot?

# CHAPTER 3

# Love the Urban Poor

## SAM WARD, DIRECTOR OF MINISTRY

*'Business as usual' for the people of God is to love and serve the poor*

The church in our nation is forever on the move. I'd love to say we are advancing, but in reality it feels more like we simply can't keep still, like an irritable child prone to fidget. We change direction at pace and call it 'new vision'. Like Tarzan, we swing wildly from strategy to strategy, as the testimonies, techniques and talents of others convince us to move on to greener grass. We swing from attractional church to missional communities, from cell church to café church and on to Messy Church without our feet touching the ground. From seeker-friendly to seeker-centred, from social action to sung worship.

I hope and pray that the desire for change reflects our desperation to reach the last, the least and the lost. However, my fear is that our church is often seeking to land in the place most appealing to the first, the finest and the found! Maybe the pace of cultural change demands that the church evolves – I have heard that standing still is as good as going backwards. But who do we leave behind in our reckless pursuit of relevance?

Interestingly, Jesus told us of one thing that would never change; one thing that would stand the course of time and exist from one generation to the next. He spoke of something that social transformation could never flee from, and cultural evolution could never shake off; an issue that affects every nation, tribe and tongue, and therefore should affect the nature of every church.

## 'THE POOR YOU WILL ALWAYS HAVE WITH YOU'

As Jesus made his final journey to Jerusalem, he stopped off for lunch at the home of Simon the leper in a place called Bethany. It was there, whilst clearly still very much living and breathing and reclining at the table, Jesus was anointed for his forthcoming burial. A woman standing close by broke an alabaster jar of expensive perfume and then poured its contents over the head of Jesus, much to the displeasure of one particular disciple. Jesus responds to Judas with these incredible words: 'The poor you will always have with you, but you will not always have me' (Matthew 26:11).

A profound moment, marked with profound words that are profoundly misunderstood. *The poor you will always have with you…* Many things will change but one thing will remain – the poor will always be around. What I find so concerning is that many in the

24

church have chosen to adopt these words as their excuse for apathy in the face of poverty: 'If Christ said that there will always be poor people, then what is the point of trying to make a difference?' they seem to say. But is this passage really a prophecy about humankind's innate inability to solve the poverty issue? Can this passage really be used to justify doing little or nothing to serve the poor? No, these words do not signify Jesus carefully lifting his church off the hook of responsibility. These words were not meant to paralyse the people of God – in fact, quite the opposite.

With those words, Jesus was highlighting his imminent departure. He would soon be gone. The people of God had only a fleeting moment to worship 'the Word made flesh' in the flesh. It was the tiniest window of opportunity within which to worship the Emmanuel, God incarnate, before it was back to business as usual. And 'business as usual' for the people of God is to love and serve the poor. The poor will always be with you, so you will always have a responsibility to serve them. They are your people. They are your neighbours so you must love them as you love yourself.

## MAKING POVERTY PERSONAL

Listen to Deuteronomy 15:7-11…

> 'If anyone is poor among your fellow Israelites in any of the towns of the land the Lord your God is giving you, do not be hard-hearted or tight-fisted toward them. Rather, be open-handed and freely lend them whatever they need. Be careful not to harbour this wicked thought: "The seventh year, the year for cancelling debts, is near," so that you

do not show ill will toward the needy among your fellow Israelites and give them nothing. They may then appeal to the Lord against you, and you will be found guilty of sin. Give generously to them and do so without a grudging heart; then because of this the Lord your God will bless you in all your work and in everything you put your hand to. There will always be poor people in the land. Therefore I command you to be open-handed toward your fellow Israelites who are poor and needy in your land.'

As the people of God, we have become accustomed to opening our hands in worship. We lift our arms and open our hands whilst we sing anthems of praise. Yet we forget that we are called to be soft-hearted and open-handed towards the poor among us. Our people. Our neighbours.

Our heart for the urban poor is not exceptional or radical – it is essential. Our passion for those experiencing poverty does not start with a moment of divine inspiration – it starts with simple obedience. I don't believe there is a special gifting of compassion for the broken. Our heart for the poor isn't an optional extra, but an unavoidable consequence of true worship.

Tim Keller writes: 'Indifference to the poor and disadvantaged means there has not been a true grasp of our salvation by sheer grace.' You cannot love God with all your heart and not share his heart of love for others. We are compelled to act by the love that God has for the least and the lost and the last. The more I worship God, the louder I hear his voice for those rejected and abandoned.

We have a God who loves his people with such passion that he would send his only Son to be the rescue plan. We received Christ who not only associated himself with the despised and the rejected, but became so himself. We have a Saviour who not only sat among the poor but also became poor in order to save us. Our passion for the urban poor comes from God and yet it is only a shadow of the love our God has for those affected by poverty.

How can we convince God we are loving him with our best, and loving our neighbours as ourselves, whilst failing to love and serve the poor among us? One solution is to move away from the poor. If you can't alleviate the problem, you have to strive to alleviate the guilt the problem causes. We all too easily shield our eyes from seeing the poor and shelter our lives from the issues of poverty altogether.

We must make poverty personal again. Gustavo Gutierrez writes: 'You say you care about the poor? Then tell me, what are their names?' We must allow ourselves to be exposed to the harsh reality of the nation's poverty and its complexities. We need to eyeball hardship and dwell in disadvantage and not simply walk on by, hoping someone else will bring healing. Has the church become the priest on the Jericho road that fails to stop and minister to the man that was beaten to within an inch of his life?

I believe the church in our nation is failing the poor. I have spoken to many potential church planters, full of good intentions to grow churches in my city. As I enquire as to their new church location, my heart almost always drops as the same rhetoric is repeated. Churches are planted everywhere but areas of deprivation. Some come for the students, others for the coffee-drinking hipsters, but it is rare I meet anyone seeking to plant into poverty.

## REDISTRIBUTING KINGDOM RESOURCES

In 1971 Dr Julian Tudor Hart completed his research into what he termed 'The Inverse Care Law.' Tudor Hart was the first to recognise the link between health and wealth. His research proved that those with greater means are likely to receive a greater quality of healthcare. Anecdotally this is evidenced in the disparity of life expectancy between an Eden neighbourhood and that of a wealthy suburb. This trend is repeated in education: the more affluent you are, the more likely you are to receive a higher standard of school.

Sadly, I believe this trend extends to the church. Our most vibrant churches are not found in the most deprived areas of the country. The Church of England invests over 50% more per head into affluent churches. The wealthiest churches by their very nature contain the greatest levels of resourcing. Plenty of pounds and palatial properties attract the best people. Prosperity is an upward spiral; poverty is the opposite.

This is not the kingdom of God that I read about in the scriptures: a kingdom established by the one who did not see equality with God as something to be grasped. A kingdom formed by the one who emptied himself and made himself nothing. A kingdom in which the weak shame the strong. A kingdom that belongs to the poor.

The Eden Network is passionate about the redistribution of kingdom resources. We want to strengthen the local church in deprived communities. We ask people to relocate into areas of deprivation. We talk of being countercultural and opting for downward mobility. We ask people to choose the downward spiral for the sake of the least, the last and the lost. It is an honour to one of the six hundred or so people who have already made that move. I am proud to be have been a volunteer in one of our fifty or so teams that have joined the mission of God into some of our nation's hardest places. I am overjoyed that our team was tasked to plant one of the 18 churches that Eden has initiated over the years. The church in disadvantaged neighbourhoods should not be disadvantaged further by the church, and I love that Eden is playing its part in redressing the imbalance.

So why are we specifically passionate about urban poverty? It might appear that a movement named 'Eden' would be more focused on rural deprivation – that we'd be passionate about places where flowers, forests and fruit abound! But in fact we're people most passionate about the concrete jungles where grass is grown with hydroponics and fruit comes in tins! The Eden Network takes its name from our first team which was planted some 20 years ago. Wythenshawe, located in South Manchester, was built as a 'garden city', to rehouse some of Manchester's poorest residents. Providing the disadvantaged with newly built properties with gardens nicely situated on tree-lined streets had its benefits, but ripping people from their networks and neighbours and relocating them in Europe's largest council estate, dislocated from the city, was ill-advised. For many years Wythenshawe was the nation's most deprived place, right at the top of the UK Government's Indices of Deprivation for England.

Among other scriptures, Eden was inspired by Ezekiel 36:

"'This is what the Sovereign Lord says: On the day I cleanse you from all your sins, I will resettle your towns, and the ruins will be rebuilt. The desolate land will be cultivated instead of lying desolate in the sight of all who pass through it. They will say, "This land that was laid waste has become like the garden of Eden; the cities that were lying in ruins, desolate and destroyed, are now fortified and inhabited." Then the nations around you that remain will know that I the Lord have rebuilt what was destroyed and have replanted what was desolate. I the Lord have spoken, and I will do it' (vv. 33-36).

It's fascinating to me that scripture starts with a garden and ends with a city. This migration from rural to urban dwelling is happening at a greater speed than at any other point in the history of the planet. Urbanisation is unrelenting with an estimated 190,000 new city dwellers added to the world's urban population *every day*. The UN forecasts that today's urban population of 3.2 billion will rise to nearly 5 billion by 2030, with 2 billion of them living in city slums. The poorest people in the world are now found in cities. As cities continue to grow, the issues of urban poverty are set to increase.

Eden is passionate about urban areas of deprivation because that's where the greatest concentration of those facing poverty are found. God comes close to the broken-hearted and he does that by sending his people. Our movement of incarnational relocators is just getting started. If all this stirs your heart, perhaps you'll pray with me, 'Here I am Lord, send me' (Isaiah 6:8).

# CHAPTER 4

# Never Forget the Poorest of the Poor

## GARY SMITH, MESSAGE WALES DIRECTOR

*'Whoever is generous to the poor lends to the LORD, and he will repay him for his deed' (Proverbs 19:15)*

One of the great things about being part of The Message is the wonderful people from all over the world God calls to share his heart with us. One of those is Pat Pierce who came to Manchester in 2001 and told Andy, 'The Lord has seen your heart for urban youth and he's pleased with it. But today he says, "Never forget the poorest of the poor."'

That simple statement set our movement on a trajectory that we are still on today. We tithe our unrestricted income to projects which share our heart for the poorest of the poor, particularly in the developing world. One of the greatest joys for Andy and the Exec team is to decide how to spend the tithe.

The Message has mission as a core part of our DNA, and you might reasonably imagine that many of us preach regularly from that famous verse, John 3:16: 'For God so loved the world that he gave his one and only Son, that whoever believes in him shall not perish but have eternal life.' But maybe, if we're being honest, we quote a little less frequently from 1 John 3:16 and the verses which follow…

> 'This is how we know what love is: Jesus Christ laid down his life for us. And we ought to lay down our lives for our brothers and sisters. If anyone has material possessions and sees a brother or sister in need but has no pity on them, how can the love of God be in that person? Dear children, let us not love with words or speech but with actions and in truth' (vv. 16-18).

## CAPTIVATED BY COMPASSION

In 1998, I was tour manager and booking agent for Rebecca St James, a Christian recording artist who was massive at that time. I was invited to a lunch by her UK record label to meet a gentleman called Tony Neeves. He had the huge task of helping to launch the child sponsorship charity Compassion in the UK. As he shared his heart about the transformation that can happen when a child has the cost of their education, medical and social needs met by a British person giving the equivalent of the price of a Mars bar every day, I was hooked. Where could I sign?

At the first opportunity, I sponsored a young man called Jairo from Mexico. He became like another member of our family, though we never met him. We prayed for him every day, wrote to him regularly and chipped in a bit extra for his birthday and at Christmas. My wife and children have sponsored many other children since then. Not only that, the ministry I co-founded, Ignite (now Message Wales), became ambassadors for Compassion using every opportunity to encourage youth groups, churches and individuals to sponsor kids.

Rebecca St James and many other artists we worked with shared about Compassion at their gigs over the years. A personal highlight for me was standing on the stage at the Belfast Odyssey Arena just before Michael W Smith headlined the show. I interviewed Debbie, Smitty's wife, and Peace, a former Compassion sponsored child. There and then we encouraged people to commit to sponsoring a child. After the gig I was wandering the corridors of the arena when the local Compassion manager approached me, beaming. That night 354 children had been sponsored!

The next day I was backstage at the Royal Albert Hall in London. A capacity crowd filled the plush velvet seats of the most famous concert hall in the world. Tony Neeves came to me and said, 'Whatever you did last night, do it again.' Talk about pressure! As I stepped out, I prayed. We did the interview, and I introduced the promotional video that we always played just before we asked people to sponsor a child. Behind me an advert for a Christian movie started playing – they had cued up the wrong video! Fearing we were going to lose the moment, I went straight to encouraging people to rescue kids from poverty in Jesus' name by sponsoring a child that night. Whilst not a total car crash, it felt a bit shambolic.

I left the platform and went to my seat and watched the show. At the end of the night I skulked up to the Compassion stand. Expecting the worst, I asked how many children had been sponsored. The answer? Once again, 354! When you experience something like that, you know it's the Lord. He loves the heart of Compassion.

## OUR HEART FOR HAITI

Joining the Message movement was made all the sweeter for me by the fact that The Message loves the ministry of Compassion, too. As an organisation, we sponsor a Compassion child for every single employee and many sponsor additional children out of their own funds. There must be well over 100 children who receive letters and gifts from our wonderful staff. Most of them live in Haiti, perhaps the poorest country in the Western hemisphere. For years now Andy Hawthorne has been visiting Haiti, not only to meet many of the sponsored children but to see the incredible work undertaken by Compassion to make their lives better. On these trips we get to see first-hand the effectiveness of the work of Compassion and how the Lord is using the money to bring lasting change.

In 2010, a devastating earthquake shook Haiti. The epicentre was in the capital city, Port-au-Prince, and the impact affected more than three million people. Many died; of those that survived, many more were injured, homeless and traumatised. People living in makeshift shelters, having lost their homes, were further affected when looting reached epidemic proportions, particularly as thousands of prisoners escaped the capital's prison. Medicines became scarce, and Andy and

Manchester church leader Anthony Delaney were invited to join a team led by Justin Dowds, now Compassion's UK CEO, to carry kilos of medical supplies into the nation.

The scenes they witnessed were horrific. Andy writes:

> I recall travelling around the devastated country and seeing apocalyptic scenes and destruction beyond belief. In one makeshift graveyard alone were believed to be 100,000 bodies. The scene that will be forever engraved on my heart was Leogane, which was at the epicentre of the earthquake. In the baking heat, with the smell of rotting flesh everywhere, we met a pastor called Mennard, who was a former Compassion sponsored child. He had lost members of his family and dozens of his church members. He had a brush in his hand and was sweeping up in the ruins of his church building and school. He had a haunted expression and was wearing a cap that said 'Jesus is my boss'.
>
> It really felt dark and I almost felt like I could hear the demons' laughter. Yet I have had the privilege since then to travel back to Haiti and with our help and the help of many others, Pastor Mennard, like so many brave Christians across Haiti, has rebuilt his church and school with even better earthquake-proof buildings and continues to pour his life into the last, least and lost in Leogane.

This beautiful kingdom partnership meant that in a small but significant way we could assist many of the poorest people to begin the recovery from this disaster. Our tithe fund not only helped with the earthquake disaster recovery, it has also funded vocational skills training, built latrines, paid for medical interventions and funded three students through Compassion's leadership development programme. For us, it is a strategic kingdom partnership.

## BEAUTY FROM ASHES

Some disasters can be described as natural, while others are caused by people. In both kinds, God can shine his light.

On July 7, 2005, three terrorist bombs exploded in London, killing 52 people and injuring a further 700. On that day a man named Prasad, a pastor from the Indian city of Rajahmundry, was prevented from attending a conference in the English capital because train lines into London were closed in the aftermath of the incident. In a panic, he got on a bus to Cardiff to meet with the only person he knew in the UK – an Indian student called Johnson. When he phoned home to tell people he was safe and now in Wales, a pastor from his home town gave him the number of a Christian youth organisation there called Ignite. He called my co-founder Nigel, who met him and invited him for lunch.

Satan always overplays his hand. From an outrageous act of destruction, the Lord was about to release an outpouring of his kingdom that would not only bless some of the poorest people in India but also the countless people from the UK and US who have since travelled there to witness first-hand the impact of the work.

Three months after first meeting Prasad, Nigel was on a plane to India. He knew that God was telling him to help build a school for Dalit children. Formerly known as the 'untouchable caste', these kids really are the poorest of the poor. After a few days Nigel texted me saying he was preaching in a church which consisted of six posts, a roof and a mud floor. It would cost £800 to put down a concrete floor and build brick walls. I knew Ignite did not have the money but I sensed the Lord telling us to do it anyway. Six weeks later, the first 'Ignite church' was opened. When you read this I am not sure how many we will have, but I do know we will not stop sending money until we have built at least 50. In the West we often say buildings are not important. In India, where the culture is used to having a temple for worship, churches are launch pads for evangelism. Most churches will double in size from when we lay the cornerstone to completing the build, usually in a period of about three months. Still more will come to faith when we officially open the building and we feed the whole village and preach the gospel. It's a beautiful thing!

So now we have churches (including one in the middle of a leprosy colony which we also help feed and clothe), an English-speaking high school with 350 pupils and a 20-bed children's home, all for some of the poorest children in India who would not get educated unless people in the West gave generously. At The Message we love our increased involvement supporting this work.

It's also been a privilege to support individual evangelists in sharing the gospel in some of the world's poorest places. James Koroma was born in Sierra Leone to a Muslim family. When he moved to the UK his life was turned upside down when he accepted Jesus as his Saviour. When we first met James he was known as Abdul and he was one of the intake of 2015 to our Message Academy, the year-long training course we run in Manchester. After being with us a year he began to share his desire to return periodically to Sierra Leone to preach the gospel. How could we not support the dream of a young guy going back to the gangs of Freetown to share the story of his radical encounter with Jesus? Each time he reports back we rejoice in the salvation stories as he describes the encounters he has had on the streets, in schools, churches and at concerts.

The Bible reminds us, 'Whoever is generous to the poor lends to the LORD, and he will repay him for his deed' (Proverbs 19:15, ESV). We know this to be true as God continues to demonstrate to us year in, year out. For us it's a no-brainer. So for as long as people give to The Message, we will keep giving to the poorest of the poor.

# CHAPTER 5

# Believe the Problem Can Become the Solution

## TIM TUCKER, MESSAGE SOUTH AFRICA DIRECTOR

*The worst offenders can become the best evangelists if we love them well*

Cape Town, South Africa, is widely agreed to be one of the most beautiful cities in the world. Nestling around the magnificence of Table Mountain, the beaches bustle with international visitors who enjoy the amazing climate and the many attractions that the city has to offer. But just a few miles away from the tourist hotspots and the wealthy suburbs, there is a completely different reality that faces hundreds of thousands of Cape Town's residents on a daily basis.

Cape Town is one of the most socio-economically divided cities in the world – a consequence of the Apartheid-era government's policy of separating people based upon the colour of their skin. Those who live in the impoverished sprawling townships and neighbourhoods of the Cape Flats are faced with the challenges of poverty, poor education and high unemployment. The area suffers from extreme levels of violent crime, which is perpetuated as rival gangs fight for territory. Young people growing up here are easily enticed into joining gangs which provide a pseudo-community that aids their survival and gives the appearance of security. Most dangerous of all are the 'numbers gangs', prison-based gangs that infiltrate and influence gang activity back in the 'hood. Gangsterism is rife in communities across Cape Town and is a barrier to the gospel that needs to be addressed.

## STEVE'S STORY: DESTRUCTION TO DISCIPLESHIP

Young men like Steve Sam are the face of the problems in Cape Town. But as we know from The Message's work globally, they also carry the potential to be the answer. Having been involved in gang activity from a young age, Steve was sentenced to 22 years in prison while he was still a teenager. To survive in prison he continued his life as a gangster – including the numbers gangs. The normal narrative for a man like Steve was that he remains in the gangs and floats in and out of prison during a life of destructive activity.

The Message launched in Cape Town in 2014, seeking to answer the questions, 'What would it take to reach a young person like Steve, caught up in gang activity?' and 'How do we move them from being part of the problem to being a testimony for the solution?' We specifically felt that God was calling us to develop a strategy around reaching prison-based gang members with the gospel, discipling them effectively, and providing an environment for them to flourish in faith and life. As we often say at The Message, 'The only thing Jesus is counting is disciples.'

We got to know Steve while he was still in prison. Having made a commitment to Christ, he joined our in-prison Message Enterprise Programme which seeks to help offenders prepare for life beyond prison. In fact, reaching men in prison with the gospel is the easy part – but that's just the beginning. Our intention was not only to disciple and prepare Steve and another 25 young men in the programme for life beyond prison, but to also provide opportunities for them to be integrated into a supportive community, earn a living and continue to grow in faith. We recognised that we needed to develop a *through-care process* that would enable young men like Steve to not just survive, but to flourish beyond prison. Critically, just as gang activity is a barrier to the gospel in communities across Cape Town, so the practical issues of housing and work are barriers to individuals like Steve from being able to continue in their faith and lead Christ-centred productive lives. So, over the last few years, we have developed a process that enables us to provide ongoing support and opportunity for young men beyond prison.

On the day he was released, our prison team met Steve at the parole office. As his parents had passed away, Steve was offered a place in our halfway home which is in a community with a resident Eden team. Steve was assigned a mentor who continued to disciple him; he started attending one of our partner churches, and we were able to offer Steve a job. Today, Steve is spearheading our gang-awareness programme called REFOCUS which aims to empower youth at risk to make positive choices and escape the clutches of the gangs. REFOCUS is centred on a curriculum that Steve himself has helped to write.

Steve's is a great story. He is now serving God and having a huge influence across the city. We have others like Steve working in our micro-business, Gangstar Enterprises. Through providing this holistic support we are seeing former gangsters becoming Gangstars and living Christ-centred productive lives. Our goal is for young men like Steve to become strong Christian leaders in the city, impacting the next generation of young people to reject the gangs, and follow Christ.

## TRANSFORMING GANGSTERS INTO GANGSTARS

As we have pursued making this dream a reality, we have learned a number of critical principles that shape our approach to mission if we want to see gangsters become Gangstars. Whether it's in Manchester, Vancouver or Cape Town, we believe that if we follow this model, we can give the most broken young men and women the best possible chance of flourishing.

### ONE – See the potential

In order for gangsters to become Gangstars, we need to see the potential in every gang member to be transformed through encountering Jesus Christ. Unsurprisingly, there is a very negative narrative that exists around gangsters in Cape Town. They cause devastation to communities on a daily basis. Even while writing this, I heard another incident of a child being caught in the crossfire as she was simply playing in her front yard. These are daily incidents and cause many people to lose hope that gang members can ever change. Even young people themselves have lost hope.

One 16-year-old Cape Town resident I met told me: 'Gang life is like a religion to my family. My father and grandfather were in gangs and they have done time in jail – I will probably end up there as well. It is the way of life here; it is where you learn about respect and get status.' But we have faith that God can change the hardest heart and we believe that in every young person there is potential for them to become an 'oak of righteousness, a planting of the LORD for the display of his splendour' (Isaiah 61:3b).

We want to see the narrative change from hopelessness to hope, from unbelief to faith and from destructive patterns to kingdom influence. It starts with us having faith and believing that God loves each young person and has a redemptive plan for their life.

## TWO – Go deep

Given the depth of the challenges that our young people are facing, we need to avoid shallow responses to what is happening in society. Because we see the potential in each young person, we share the gospel broadly and anticipate a response. But that is just the beginning. Jesus called us to make disciples, and the road of discipleship requires deep engagement with people over a long period of time – particularly if they come from messy and dysfunctional backgrounds.

The implication for us at The Message is that we also need to be an organisation of depth and substance. Young people from broken backgrounds quickly sense if we are offering them shallow and superficial responses. It is imperative that our Message team are deeply engaged in the Word and are growing in maturity as Christians. Additionally, we need to be aware of what is happening in society and making biblically informed responses in order that we can speak prophetically into the context which is cultivating the gang culture.

In Ezekiel 47, God gave the prophet a vision of a river flowing from the restored temple in Jerusalem. As the river flowed out from the altar and away from the temple, it deepened until it became a mighty river. The river flowed into the Dead Sea and resulted in the transformation of the saltiest sea on the planet into a freshwater paradise of abundant life. This vision gives us a metaphor for the correlation between depth and fruitfulness. As we seek to disciple former gang members and ensure they have a deep biblical foundation for their life, so we can anticipate that they themselves will live fruitful lives.

One of the baristas in our coffee shop, Xola, is an example of this principle. He came to Christ in prison and received a great foundation for his faith through attending an Alpha course. Upon release from prison, he continued to grow in his faith as a committed member of his local church. We were able to organise his barista training and gave him a job at our Gangstar Café. He now works hard to earn his living, but on the weekends he is out in his old neighbourhoods preaching the gospel, leading Alpha groups and mentoring young people. This is the kind of fruit that we begin to see when we go deep!

**THREE – Provide a place to flourish**

Xola's story is also evidence of our third principle: that we need to provide an environment for former prisoners and gang members to flourish. At The Message we have numerous innovative programmes that we have initiated over the years but they are unified by our central objective of raising up urban heroes who can become champions for the gospel. However, it is nearly impossible for a former gang member with a criminal record to remain strong in their faith if they are not part of a supportive community and if they are not able to provide for themselves and their families.

Father Gregory Boyle, founder of Homeboy Industries in California says, 'Nothing stops a bullet like a job.' He should know, as he's employed hundreds of former gang members from the toughest housing projects in LA! Our company in South Africa is called Gangstar Enterprises. It too is a redemptive brand that seeks to establish a platform for former gang members to flourish in faith and life through providing work experience and jobs. One goal of Gangstar Enterprises is to address the stigma that young people with criminal records face when seeking to find work. We want to demonstrate that people, as Christ enables them, can turn their lives around and become productive members of society. Our task at Gangstar Enterprises is to give them that first opportunity that no one else will give.

Jerome is one such beneficiary of the environment we're developing. He completed our Message Enterprise Programme and then had the opportunity to do work experience with Gangstar Enterprises upon release from prison, while living in one of our halfway homes. Having adjusted to life outside prison, he then received a job opportunity with a partner company that is willing to employ our Gangstars. After flourishing at work, he was then approached by City Mission to spearhead their football in the community coaching programme. Jerome is passionate about football, is now working in his dream job while impacting young people from tough neighbourhoods – and is constantly on Facebook giving glory to God! He is flourishing because of our three-pronged approach: we saw the potential, we went deep in discipleship, and we were able to provide an environment of holistic support.

## ANYTHING IS POSSIBLE WITH GOD

'Gangsters to Gangstars' is one of those things that can seem impossible to man – but is possible with God. The key verse God gave us when we launched Gangstar Enterprises is Philippians 2:15-16, which is our desire for all our Gangstars: 'so that you may become blameless and pure, children of God without fault in a warped and crooked generation. Then you will shine among them like stars in the sky as you hold firmly to the word of life.'

We believe that this is just the beginning for The Message in South Africa. We are praying that more gangsters like Steve, Xola and Jerome will become Gangstars who unashamedly serve Jesus Christ and share his love with many others across the city.

We believe that God is calling Message South Africa to be a catalyst for new South African stories. Our dream is to see a kingdom ripple effect that will eradicate the negative influence of gangsterism and see new gangs emerge – gangs full of Gangstars who serve Christ and bring a positive gospel impact to all corners of Cape Town and beyond.

## CHAPTER 6

# Have Faith for Finances

## COLLETTE DALLAS, FINANCE DIRECTOR

*The finances of a faith ministry are a very spiritual matter*

People often say to me, 'Collette, you're not a typical accountant!' I take this as a great compliment. Yes, I have over 25 years' experience in the accountancy world, in practice, commerce and the charity sector. And yes, I have accumulated plenty of accounting qualifications during that time. What I have learned, though, is that experience and qualifications don't really prepare you for being the Finance Director of a fast-growing Christian ministry. Both are very important, obviously. But equally important is the need for a large dose of faith for finances.

Before coming to The Message Trust, I had the privilege of serving in a ministry called Kingdom Faith where I was schooled in the principles of faith under the tutelage of Colin Urquhart, and two of his best leaders, Judith Butler and Jonathan Croft. This is where I first learned to walk in faith, and in faith for finances.

I learnt that faith is based on a living relationship, not a theory. It is a lifestyle birthed in intimacy with the living God, the loving Father of Heaven, through the death and resurrection of the Lord Jesus Christ. He is a God upon whom we can trust, we can totally depend, and we can believe with all our heart to keep his every word.

When it comes to finances, my belief is that everything in this world belongs to God and that means his resources are unlimited. I believe that as we trust and depend on him, our loving Father, he will supply all our needs and will provide all that we need to fulfil any vision he has planted in our hearts.

## GOD'S ECONOMIC SYSTEM

During my time at The Message, I have come to appreciate more and more that God's economic system is very different from the world's. God's economic system gives vision first, and from that vision, faith is birthed. It is from this dynamic combination of vision and faith that all our works are produced. Vision inspires faith that comes from hearing the Word, and then that faith which is assurance (see Hebrews 11:1) that the Lord will do all he says he will do, inspires us in all that we do.

Faith for finances in my mind is having the assurance, the confidence, that the Lord will provide for any vision he has given to us. Without the vision birthed through scriptures like Isaiah 43 (our cornerstone scripture), Psalm 37 (Eden), and Isaiah 60 (Higher), and the faith which they inspired, The Message would not have seen the miraculous provision and breakthrough in finances that we have seen over the years, nor would we have been able to carry out the tremendous work of reaching thousands of lost and broken young people for the Lord.

So how did we apply our faith for finances? By preparing faith-filled budgets, faithfully stewarding God-given finances, constantly praying faith-filled prayers, faithfully giving to others, partnering with faithful supporters and recruiting faithful people and by being continually thankful to God for his faithfulness and provision.

## FAITH-FILLED BUDGETS AND THE 'FAITH GOAL'

In my experience, the best and most achievable budgets are when they are birthed and driven by vision, not the other way around. As my good friend Alan Morton would say, 'Budgets are a statement of faith.' God-given vision produces faith-filled budgets whose ultimate goal is to fulfil a God-given vision. For The Message, this is to reach as many lost and broken people as possible by unashamedly preaching the whole gospel of our Lord Jesus Christ.

Key ingredients of faith-filled budgets are that they account for all costs, both direct and indirect project costs. Luke 14:28 reminds us, 'Don't begin until you count the cost. For who would begin... without first calculating the cost to see if there is enough money to finish it?' Faith-filled budgets account for all income that we are certain will come in. They also account for any income that can be generated by selling services or goods, and by fundraising.

But in all faith-filled budgets, there is also the recognition that some of the income that is needed will only come in through the miraculous provision of the Lord. That is what I have affectionately termed over my 15 years at The Message as our 'Faith Goal.' I call it that because seeing that money coming in month after month requires faith – a lot of faith! It is the gap that only God in his goodness can fill. Historically, about a third of The Message's budgeted income has been this Faith Goal income.

## FAITHFUL STEWARDSHIP

Another key for having faith for finances is having a biblical perspective of finances, where we believe that everything, including money, belongs to God – and we are called to be good stewards. It is our belief that he will release his unlimited resources to those that share his heart and vision, and seek to steward his resources wisely. I love what Kent Wilson from the Acton Institute said about stewardship. He calls it 'the faithful and efficient management of resources that belong to another in order to achieve the owner's objectives.'

I spent my first few years at The Message working with the Finance team and all the organisation's budget holders to put in place systems and internal controls to create greater ownership, accountability and compliance. I felt it was key that all budget holders had a good understanding of their role and responsibilities as stewards of God's finances.

During this season I always felt very strongly that we were preparing The Message for a great release of finances that the Lord wanted to bring to us, once he could trust us to handle the money wisely. In 1 Corinthians 4:2, the Apostle Paul writes, 'Now it is required that those who have been given a trust must prove faithful.' I believe that this is just as true for ministries like The Message as it is for individual believers.

## FAITH-FILLED PRAYER

It is important to remember everything must be underpinned with a strong culture of intercessory prayer. For many years I have had the privilege of working alongside Andy in overseeing the prayer life of the Message staff, supported by its prayer team. I can truly say that without faith-filled prayer, all our efforts would have been totally futile. The revivalist John Wesley emphasised the importance of faith and prayer when he said that 'God does nothing on earth except in answer to believing prayer.' The Bible says, in Hebrews 11:6, 'Without faith it is impossible to please God.'

Our faith for finances – mine, Andy's, the whole staff's – has been fuelled by our believing prayer and our trust in the Bible and the God of the Bible. Ultimately this comes down to lives that pursue him and his purposes, and that earnestly desire to walk in holiness and greater intimacy with him.

The finances of a faith ministry are a very spiritual matter and it is an area when the enemy often attacks us by assaulting those in leadership, in oversight and in administration of finances. Over the years our prayers for finances have resisted fear, worry and self-concern and have been focused on being thankful and being full of faith in the Lord who has faithfully shown us, time and time again, that he is our good Father, our provider. He can and is willing to give us our daily bread and 'supply all our need according to his riches in glory by Christ Jesus' (Philippians 4:19, KJV). I think that it is especially worth noting how essential having a positive confession and faith-filled speech about the goodness of God and his faithfulness have been key to expelling fear and encouraging our faith for finances.

From very early on in my time at The Message, the Finance team and I have sent out a monthly email to inform staff of the extra general funds, after accounting for known income and costs, that we need to come in to continue our work and pay every bill on time – in other words, the Faith Goal for that month. This encourages everyone to play their part in praying for the 'daily bread' of the ministry. We have consistently done this for almost 15 years.

## FAITHFULLY GIVING TO OTHERS

Another key for faith for finances is sharing God's heart to give, and trusting him to provide you with more than enough so that you can give to others. A couple of my favourite scriptures on giving are:

> 'Be generous: Invest in acts of charity. Charity yields high returns. Don't hoard your goods; spread them around. Be a blessing to others' (Ecclesiastes 11:1-2, MSG)

> 'God is able to bless you abundantly, so that in all things at all times, having all that you need, you will abound in every good work' (2 Corinthians 9:8)

I have learnt in particular from my time at Kingdom Faith that you must always plan to give, especially when preparing faith-filled budgets. So for the last 15 years we have planned to give 10% of all our income (out of unrestricted funds) to other organisations that share a similar heart and similar objectives for reaching the lost and broken, and for caring for the poor.

We have on many occasions asked The Message staff to make suggestions as to who we should give to, and I have to say my second favourite part of our Executive team meetings (after all the wonderful stories of salvation have been shared) is deciding how much to give away to others. We do this with great joy.

Over the last 15 years we have increased our giving to causes close to our heart from £8,000 in 2002-2003 to £300,000 by the end of this financial year. At our annual vision days, when Andy shares how much we have given in the last financial year, there are always gasps of amazement and great rejoicing. What an honour to share in God's heart to give!

## PARTNERING WITH FAITHFUL PEOPLE

A great encouragement to my faith for finances are the thousands of faithful supporters who sacrificially give to partner with the Lord in seeing his purposes fulfilled through the work of The Message. I am always blown away by the generosity of our supporters. We could not sustain this work without them. They are truly the hands and feet of Christ. And I'm pleased to say this generosity starts with our own staff. At a recent prayer day Gavin Calver said, 'Don't expect people to give to your ministry if you don't give yourself.' I know for sure that every member of staff could confidently say they do give into the work of The Message – wonderful!

Another important key to having faith for finances is to surround yourself with people of faith. As well as being blessed with a fantastic CEO and Exec team, The Message has a faith-filled team of trustees. But also crucially important is to have faithful hands-on stewards of the finances, the Accounts team. This requires a very special group of people. I didn't come to The Message for a job – I was sent from a fantastic ministry because I felt called to the vision of reaching the lost. It has been vital that the Message Accounts and Fundraising teams have that same call. So I am truly grateful for those the Lord has called to serve alongside me.

## REMEMBERING TO BE THANKFUL AT ALL TIMES

I have always loved the gratitude of The Message staff when the money comes in. There have always been shouts of joy, often tears, and sometimes very silly dancing! We always take time to stop and thank God and remember his lavish faithfulness to us. As it says in Deuteronomy 8, it is so important to stop, remember and thank the Lord for his goodness: 'But remember the LORD your God, for it is he who gives you the ability to produce wealth, and so confirms his covenant, which he swore to your ancestors, as it is today' (Deuteronomy 8:18).

We have so many beautiful testimonies of God's provision to remember. Back in 2008, we needed around £80,000 to pay our staff salary bill. A donor rang promising to transfer some money into our account (he didn't tell us the amount at the time). Later, after much prayer and thanksgiving, we checked our bank account and noticed he had given £100,000. Amazing! But then we noticed another line underneath it – another £100,000 had been given! Andy immediately rang the donor to thank him for the £100,000 and to inform him of the mistake of the additional amount. But the donor told us to keep it! Amazingly, in one day, God provided all we needed and much more. You can imagine the shouts of jubilation when Andy told the team!

The Message Enterprise Centre (MEC) took our need for faith for finances to a whole new level. Although our prisons ministry teams were seeing many young people becoming Christians and being baptised in young offenders' institutions, for many years we had been heartbroken by how many we saw turning back to their old lifestyles once they left prison. There was an enormous need for a new model of mentoring and support for ex-offenders in our city. The MEC was our answer: a place where the young people we had worked with in prison could receive training with qualifications, a real job, and huge amounts of support from our dedicated team. We dreamed of converting a derelict property adjacent to Message HQ in Manchester into a dynamic business hub where this could take place. But that would cost in excess of £1.2m, and we didn't have a single penny in the account to purchase the land, let alone refurbish the building.

But in faith, we pursued the property – and against all the odds, every penny was raised. Since the MEC was launched, we have seen a dramatic turnaround in reoffending with the young people we work with, and many are today growing in discipleship and serving local churches. Based on our calculations, within just three years of opening its doors the MEC saved the public purse £1.2m in court costs alone – not to mention all the associated costs of policing and welfare!

More recently, in June 2017, we faced a historically large Faith Goal. Although our annual Urban Hero Awards event was approaching fast, we knew from past experience that it would be unlikely to raise enough to cover our immediate needs, let alone our plans to expand our work in the MEC, the regions and overseas. We urgently needed

God to come through for us. As always, we did everything that we could do practically in terms of fundraising, but also, and most importantly, we prayed, expecting God to come through for us and provide what we needed to fulfil his vision.

Amazingly, over £250,000 came in on the night of the event. A donor who only confirmed attendance on the day of the event put in the largest single gift, and the last £4,000 that we needed was given by someone who was literally leaving the building when the final appeal was made! So the Lord provided all that we needed to smash the Faith Goal, to give some money away to others, and to carry out our plans for expansion. What an amazing God we serve!

## NOT A TYPICAL ACCOUNTANT

It has been a great privilege to be at The Message over the last decade and a half. I have learnt so much about the faithfulness of God who is worthy of all our thanks and praise. So I take it as a compliment that people think of me as 'not a typical accountant.' I would love to be known first as a woman of prayer and faith. My hope is that as my faith has been challenged and grown over the years, it will have inspired others in their journey, and in their trust in the Lord and in his Word. He is the Faithful One.

# CHAPTER 7

# Don't Take Yourself Too Seriously

## ANDY HAWTHORNE, FOUNDER AND CEO

*He must become greater, we must become less*

More than anything, I reckon this book is about finding out what we can do to attract God's attention and build a firm foundation for a life or ministry of maximum fruitfulness. I believe taking mission and prayer seriously, having a heart for the poor, living a faith-filled life and trying to do it all in humility are basic and non-negotiable things, for instance.

So, you might be wondering, is 'Don't take yourself too seriously' really worth a whole chapter?

Yes, in my opinion, it is – especially as I look at the carnage and hurt that has been caused by ministers and leaders who through the years have taken themselves far too seriously, and actually started to believe their own hype. That's why at The Message we like to say, 'We take not taking ourselves too seriously, very seriously!'

For instance, I make fun of my team regularly. One sure way you can know you are my friend and I like you is that I feel able to involve you in a bit of gentle ribbing. I deliberately encourage people on my teams to gently make fun of one another and I hope I embrace it when they make fun of me (which they do often!) Why? Because I've seen leaders who can't laugh at themselves and are constantly on the defensive, who simply can't be told they are wrong. To be honest, it makes me cringe.

Being able to laugh at yourself is just one sign that you're taking yourself too seriously. There are plenty of others. For instance, people who take themselves too seriously often have a difficult time admitting they are wrong, even if they are! In arguments they always have to have the last word, or feel the need to justify themselves for having the argument in the first place. Another sign is that they rarely give compliments to others, or find it hard to find good things to say about them.

## MAN-PLEASER OR GOD-PLEASER?

Worst of all is the trap of self-promotion and obsessing over how you look to others. We all fall into the trap of being man-pleasers, to a greater or lesser extent.

I remember when I was 19 years of age and this beautiful blonde girl called Michele Jones joined our youth group in Cheadle. One day we all went out to this amazing house in Alderley Edge with a swimming pool, and I figured this was my chance to impress Michele. So I put my trunks on, held my stomach in, and tried to look as buff as possible. And in front of all the girls, first into the pool, I attempted an athletic backflip dive.

It didn't go well. I smacked my face on the floor of the pool. I remember being under the water, thinking, 'I can taste blood! And I never want to come up!' I was trying to look cool but I ended up looking ridiculous. As so often happens when you go down that route, I ended up flat on my face.

And I still do it now. Nearly four decades later, I'm still worried what people think of me, if I'm honest. At the end of talks, I still find myself wondering, 'Is anybody going to say that was any good?' When the latest conference publicity comes out, I'm looking to check if my picture is the same size as everyone else's. I want things that are written about me to be as flattering as possible. But this ego is destructive. Proverbs 29:25 says, 'Fear of man will prove to be a snare, but whoever trusts in the Lord is kept safe.'

Seeking man's approval is a trap. I travel around a lot, speaking in different settings, and I have been introduced in some very over-the-top ways – as 'the man of God' or even, 'the mighty man of God'! I know this can come from a good heart because people want to express honour, but I'm realistic that this is simply because I lead a ministry and because I'm about to do a talk! For me, the real mighty men (and women) of God, are our Eden teams and prison workers who anonymously lay down their lives for the sake of the lost and broken, day in, day out.

So I need to stay aware of the effect these words can have on me. I get the sense that if this kind of praise and flattery isn't like water off a duck's back to me then I could quickly become a bit jumped-up and tedious. It's important to have recognition for what we do, and I get more than enough, but the real praise we should be looking for is Jesus' 'Well done, good and faithful servant' on the final day. In other words, the praise we should really be chasing is up there, not down here. We need to be God-pleasers, not man-pleasers.

## TAKING SERVING SERIOUSLY

Jesus himself was the perfect role model of living for an 'audience of One.' Surely, as the person who spoke the whole earth into being, it would have been reasonable for him to expect a bit of service and respect when he became flesh and visited the planet he had made! But instead, he constantly took on the role of a servant, even washing his disciples' smelly feet as an example that we should follow, and teaching that will be blessed if we can be similarly servant-hearted. I want to experience the kind of blessing that comes from having that favour of God on my life. I believe that comes as we take the gospel seriously – but not ourselves.

Michael Baughen is a former Bishop of Chester, and as such would have all kinds of people address him as 'Lord Bishop' and other fancy titles. He admitted that he also quite liked dressing up in the outrageous bishops' robes (which to be fair, are about as far from the Carpenter of Nazareth's garb as you could possibly get). So in order to keep him grounded, he would always keep a small piece of towel in his pocket to remind him that he was here to serve and not be served, and that he, as the leader, needed to constantly work out what it looked like to wash other disciples' feet.

I get the feeling that the reason that Jesus was able to say of John the Baptist that up to that point 'among those born of women there has not risen anyone greater' (Matthew 11:11), was that he didn't believe his hype that he was the new Elijah, or the prophet they had all been waiting for. John's life and ministry were defined by his conviction that 'He [Jesus] must become greater, I must become less' (John 3:30), and when it was time to give away two of his own disciples to Jesus' ministry, namely Simon and Andrew, he did so unhesitatingly.

Taking yourself a lot less seriously can actually be massively freeing – as you have a whole lot less to live up to! It helps you to see the humour in situations, find silver linings amid clouds, and navigate your way through life's ups and downs and curve balls. When things go wrong, if our natural defence mechanism is to throw a hissy fit then our home, church or workplace won't be a happy place. If we can laugh at ourselves, though – and in the process realise and accept some of our flaws and mistakes – then a much more productive, fun-filled atmosphere is possible.

## KEEPING EACH OTHER HUMBLE

The Message is home to some incredibly talented and creative mission teams who often perform in front of large numbers of screaming young people. Even though the object of these gigs is always to create a clear platform for the gospel, there will still be a number of these young people who love to tell our bands for hours after how awesome they are, whilst desperately seeking selfies and autographs. This little bit of fame can actually be very bad for the soul, and unless the guys and girls are really rooted in Jesus, they can start slipping down the slope of pride.

We simply can't afford for this to happen. The Bible repeatedly says that God opposes the proud and gives grace to the humble – and I know for sure which one I want. One of our best strategies for counteracting this is to not take ourselves too seriously – so if you're one of our talented creatives, get ready, because almost certainly you are in for a serious bout of mickey-taking!

In all this there needs to be sensitivity, of course, and we are not trying to hurt each other. Some people are more thin-skinned than others and we need to take this into account in all our humour. We do, however, want to make sure we do God's work God's way, and for sure, God is keen that we realise that it really is all about him and that without him, we can do nothing of any true worth.

# CHAPTER 8

# Lead with Humility and the Opposite Spirit

## CARL BEECH, DEPUTY CEO

*Understanding how blessed we have been by God changes the way we interact with one another*

At The Message we like to think of ourselves as 'mates on a mission.' But this, like most things, is easier said than done. It takes effort to foster a true sense of family and keep this combined with a sense of purpose in our work. It means we need to stay tight as a team, no matter what. For us, leading and living with the 'opposite spirit' is core to the way we interact toward each other, our partner ministries, individuals and organisations.

Allow me to give you a practical example...

A few years ago I had a very undramatic crash in my car. It was nearly Christmas and I was about a quarter of a mile from home. It was dark, it was raining, I was in a queue of traffic, and I was looking out of the window. But it was the wrong window – I was looking out of the side window when I should've been looking at the traffic! And then the inevitable happened. The car in front of me moved off, I pulled away as well, then the car in front stalled and I rolled gently into the back of it.

This was a very low-speed accident and really there shouldn't have been much damage, apart from the fact that the car I rolled into was a 1989 Vauxhall Nova. The Vauxhall Nova was built like a tank with a rubber bumper the size of Wales. The front end of my much newer car ever so gently nudged underneath the bumper of the Vauxhall Nova. Of course I immediately got out, walked to the car in front, tapped on the window and said, 'I'm terribly sorry. Merry Christmas,' with a sheepish smile on my face.

'Why did you do that?' she said (the driver being a young lady).

'Honestly, because I wasn't looking,' I said.

'Well, shall we look at the damage?' she said.

'That's a good idea,' I said. And we both walked round to the back of her car together.

She had got off very lightly – her car was pretty badly beaten up anyway. In all honesty it was probably only worth about £500. She even said that as we looked at the cars together. 'I don't think my car has any damage,' she said. 'You've not been so lucky though have you?'

It's fair to say she was right. While there was no visible damage to her car, the front of mine had turned into something roughly resembling a pterodactyl. You see, my car had a high-tech feature called a crumple zone, designed to absorb impact in the event of a bad accident or to keep you safe in your car when you crash headlong into another vehicle or indeed a wall. It seemed, in fact, that on this occasion it had over-performed. Nearly the whole front end of my car was folded up into a kind of twisted sculpture. An absolute nightmare.

I was gutted about my car but relieved about hers. She agreed there wasn't any damage to her car, and we happily swapped numbers just in case. About a week went past, and I hadn't heard anything else from the young driver of the old Vauxhall Nova.

But then I got a text message which went something like this: 'I had my car professionally assessed by a mechanic, and it seems there is over £500 worth of damage to my car. But if you send me a cheque for £100 then we can forget all about it.'

Now of course, this is a classic minor scam and merely an opportunistic way of getting some easy money from someone.

So this is where living with an opposite spirit comes in. I knew I had to get a grip on my heart. What is the point in preaching a message of grace if I can't even deal with a simple issue like this? So, I put myself metaphorically into the corner and gave myself a very strong talking to. I sent her a text back so I could go down and drop her off some money. Except that I didn't write a cheque for £100, I wrote a cheque for £150 instead.

I drove around to her house, which was easy to find because I saw her undamaged car on the driveway. Anyway, I knocked, and when she came to the door I said, 'Here is the cheque you asked for, but I put extra money on it by way of an apology. Sorry again for inconveniencing you. I just want to bless you.'

'What do you mean you want to "bless me"?' she said.

'Well, it's just the way I want to live my life,' I said.

'What do you mean?' she said.

'Well, actually I'm one of those Christian type of people,' I said.

'A Christian?' she said.

'Yes,' I said, 'and I'm sorry I crashed into you.'

'Bless me?' she said.

'Yes,' I said. 'Anyway, here is the cheque – it's only an extra fifty quid but I hope it's useful coming up to Christmas with a car to repair.'

She looked at me blankly for a moment – and then sort of went a bit weirdly pale as she looked down at the cheque and saw the title 'Reverend Carl Beech.'

I'll be honest with you, part of me wanted to say something like, 'And if you steal from a man of God you could be struck down by lightning, many bad things could befall you and your family.' But of course, I didn't. Instead, I smiled sweetly, turned on my heel, strode back past her undamaged car to my pterodactyl and drove away.

Inside, I was thinking that she probably wouldn't cash the cheque. I was thinking that she would be so overcome by grace and the love of Christ that she would never be able to pay the cheque in. I was wrong. She paid the cheque in later that afternoon, going by my bank statement. But I think it was worth the risk. Let me explain.

Let's imagine a scenario. Let's pretend that I had stood my ground and refused to give her the money, instead arguing it out and pointing out the error of her thieving ways. Let's then imagine that a year or two later she encounters you, and you invite her to an Alpha course. But she turns to you and says, 'I met this Christian minister once – in fact I actually tried to rip him off. Turns out he was a total pig, a really aggressive guy.' Well, that would really shipwreck your evangelism, wouldn't it?

Alternatively, you might meet her one day and invite her to the Alpha course – and she remembers this crazy guy that she tried to rip off, but who instead confounded her. I think she's much more likely to attend an Alpha course or respond to the gospel one day because I did something crazy like give her a few extra quid. It was worth the risk. What I did there was effectively 'put a stone in her shoe' – I think she now has a permanent gospel limp. She will be wondering what on earth I was all about. I mean, who does stuff like that? I'll tell you who does stuff like that – we do!

## CHANGING THE GAME

At The Message we want to be people who live with an opposite spirit. Jesus said, when someone forces you to go a mile, go the extra mile. When someone wants your shirt, give them your cloak as well (Matthew 5:40-41). This is what we do – it's how we live our lives. It strikes me that daily we have opportunities to react to situations in a radically different way to most people.

Now, to live this way is extremely tough. It seemingly goes against every instinct. Everything in us wants justice in these sorts of situations. Everything in us wants the truth to be known. We want people to recognise the folly and error of their ways. We can't bear the fact that someone is walking around having got the upper hand over us. We can't bear the fact that we have looked weak or useless or behaved like a doormat stamped into the ground. But that's because we have lost sight of the bigger picture. The bigger picture is that our lives are all about Christ and are lived out before an audience of One.

Just think about it for a moment – it is said by Jesus, that 'the meek will inherit the earth' (Matthew 5:5). Perhaps if all of us tried to live with an opposite spirit there would be a grace revolution that could transform towns and cities.

With that in mind I'm going to list a few scenarios where the opposite spirit could really change the game. It's tough and it takes a strong and courageous heart to have the opposite spirit in the face of injustice and hurt. But that's what it is to be a follower of 'The Way.' Here are some situations that might resonate with you:

- You get an inflammatory email that you instantly want to respond to with defensive venom and correction.
- You hear a rumour or a bit of hearsay about yourself that is grossly unfair, wounding and exposing.
- Someone posts something online that offends you or isn't true. Instant response is of course available for the world to see.
- Someone stabs you in the back at work who you trusted or thought was a friend.
- Someone parks across your driveway, blocking you in.
- Someone corrects you publicly and you feel vulnerable, undermined and humiliated.
- You have a great idea for something, then someone else steals the idea and does it for themselves, claiming all the glory.
- Someone gets the credit for something you did.
- Someone takes your parking place.

The list is endless and I could go on and on and on and on. But I won't, I will just say this: think and act like one who has a Saviour and is saved by grace, then respond in a manner befitting.

My Bible tells me God made the heavens and the earth. It tells me that he made me, and that he made you. It tells me that he knows every hair on your head, every word on your tongue, and in fact every detail of your life. It tells me that he loves you and that he loves me. My Bible tells me that we only exist because of his grace. Nanosecond by nanosecond he sustains us. Should God want to shut the whole show down, he could. It is only because of his grace that you can read this, have an opinion, and have the freedom to choose how to act in any given situation. He has asked us to live and act with grace.

## THE HIGHER PATH IS THE NARROW PATH

When we truly realise just how blessed we all are to even draw another breath, it really puts into perspective how silly it is when we get the hump over minor stuff. To take the higher path (which is in fact also a very narrow path according to Jesus' teaching in Matthew 7), is to overlook an insult, to suck up an injustice, to not defend yourself, and even to speak well of those who have antagonised you or made your life difficult.

So here are my tips for living 'the Way' in response to the list above:

- Take a deep breath. Don't reply by email. Arrange to see them face-to-face.
- Overlook the insult.
- Give the benefit of the doubt, believe the best.

- Don't row online. Don't escalate things.
- Talk to the person who did it, not 15 other people.
- Be polite, ignore it if it only happens once.
- Don't just go round to tell them about the car – ask them for a meal at the same time.
- Cheer them on.
- Cheer them on again.
- Find another parking space – and pray for them.

I think I might be able to guess what you're thinking. You're thinking that's mad and a great way to become a professional doormat. You may be right, but I would rather save my emotional energy for a fight that really matters. Frankly, parking spaces, someone pulling a fast one, someone getting more recognition than me, or a rude and factually incorrect email just don't seem that important when you consider how much grace God has shown us. Besides, putting stones in people's shoes is actually quite a lot of fun.

Here's some more 'opposite spirit' choices:

- Give the benefit of the doubt.
- Practise outrageous generosity in word or deed. Be the first to pay for people. Don't quibble the bill in a group, just make up the difference.
- Lend without expecting back.
- Complain very rarely.
- Lose an argument every so often and if you are ultra-competitive, let other people win sometimes. It's good for you.

- Be gracious to all you meet and be gracious about everyone you've met behind their backs. If you slip up, apologise. If you are misunderstood, don't defend yourself.
- Associate with people who aren't like you and who challenge your 'sophistication'.
- On the ratio of listening to speaking: listen more.
- Honour and prefer others above you.
- If you find yourself jealous of someone and making comparisons, say beautiful things about them publicly.
- Do humble things.
- Do not gossip.
- Clear the air quickly.
- Ask for forgiveness when you mess up.

Living like this not only fosters a great place to work, but really pleases the Lord as well.

# CHAPTER 9

# Think Like an Entrepreneur

## ANDY HAWTHORNE, FOUNDER AND CEO

*Risk-taking and learning from failure should be in our nature*

The Message Trust started with a verse that is all about entrepreneurial thinking and innovation: 'See, I am doing a new thing... do you not perceive it?'

Of course, that verse in Isaiah 43:19 isn't just for The Message – it's a verse for every Christian, every day. God is the endlessly creative Creator, constantly coming up with new ideas in order to see the Great Commandment and the Great Commission fulfilled. Our job is to be seeking him and perceiving his new things all the time.

The entrepreneurial leaders that the church of Jesus so much needs are thinkers who never rest on their laurels and who display all the qualities of ownership and think like a CEO, whether they have that title or not. A true movement, which is what we long for The Message to become, will be a little bit messy and have entrepreneurial people all over the place – in other words people who think anything is possible and have the tenacity and get-up-and-go to work towards it. This kind of exponential, explosive thinking tends to be evident in small ministries and businesses in their early days, yet perhaps dies down as some of these initiatives grow and become a little bit safer. However, if some of the largest businesses in the world such as Apple, Virgin and Google have managed to buck this trend and have innovation and enterprise still at the heart of all they do, why shouldn't the church of Jesus, with all the help of the genius that is the Holy Spirit, be able to do even better?

Recently, I've had the opportunity to speak at a couple of Hillsong churches in Cape Town and Moscow (yes, there really is a Hillsong Church in Moscow!). It was fascinating to hear the Hillsong story. Brian and Bobbie Houston took over Hills Community Church from Brian's father, Frank, and steadily grew it over about 15 years until they had a church of around 2,000 people meeting in one location in Sydney, Australia. Much as this was good, and indeed many people might have been satisfied with that, Brian and Bobbie weren't, and they sought the Lord and prayed into what a truly world-changing movement could look like. God gave them some entrepreneurial and innovative thinking around investing in leaders who would produce leaders, multiple sites and the Hillsong sound being heard all over the world. As a result, God blessed them and Hillsong took the journey from good to great and the explosive movement that is Hillsong today was born.

The Message may be tiny compared to Hillsong, but we are constantly on the lookout for those kinds of inflection points where God brings us new revelations and suddenly, explosive things start to happen.

Originally, The Message Trust started with a band called The World Wide Message Tribe and what a funny band we were. I would rap like a demonised member of Sesame Street, alongside my friend Mark Pennells and some dancers from our church youth group. Yet I know for sure that God loved the heart and vision we had and despite the lack of talent (particularly in my department) over the next few years we were able to present the gospel to millions of people and sell hundreds of thousands of CDs which helped to fund the first few years of The Message. As time went on, we were able to attract some genuinely gifted people to join the band and I would often stand back in awe at the brilliantly talented people God had given us to perform alongside my 'Cookie Monster' rapping.

## EVERY CHALLENGE IS AN OPPORTUNITY

When it became clear that it was time for the band to finish, we were left with a bit of a problem in that we had these amazing people on our payroll who were super gifted and had great hearts but to be honest, we didn't know what to do with. This led to a beautiful bout of entrepreneurial thinking, as firstly Tim Owen came to see me with his vision for Genetik Sessions, training up young people in the creative arts, and a dream of stepping up our Message Academy to focus on multiplying evangelistic mission teams. Because entrepreneurial thinking involves extreme ownership, he even offered to go out and raise the money. This vision that God gave to Tim has grown to become one of the most fruitful things we have ever done.

Not far behind was Emma Owen, Tim's wife. She had always been the one in the band who was a magnet to young girls, and as she thought and prayed about what new thing God would have her perceive, she came up with the dream of what would become Respect Me to help young people, and in particular young girls, deal with issues of sexuality, self-image and abuse.

Also out of this season of uncertainty came the beautiful ministry of LZ7 which has grown into its own evangelistic charity, Light; a significant new women's ministry in the United States; and a huge vision for a nightclub outreach in Manchester city centre. Even though this last particular venture collapsed spectacularly, I wasn't at all dismayed because being in an entrepreneurial culture means taking risks.

At The Message we believe whatever you celebrate, you cultivate. Of course, for us this means celebrating like crazy every time we hear a story of someone becoming a Christian and turning their lives around, especially if they come from a chaotic and broken background. But it also means being on the lookout for the kind of mind-set we want to see explode the movement across the globe and making sure everybody knows they are allowed to think 'out of the box' to do more and do it better wherever they sit in the organisational structure.

## LEARNING FROM THE BEST

Taking my own responsibility seriously as a resource raiser for The Message, I regularly get the privilege of sitting down with some of the nation's top entrepreneurs to try to convince them that they should part with some of their hard-earned cash to help us to reach the least, last and lost. There are a few vital lessons I have learnt from these brilliant men and women, especially those who started out with very little:

1. They can't help thinking entrepreneurially all the time. They are always recognising new opportunities and spotting ways to exploit them. I'm convinced that being an entrepreneur can be caught and developed but it's great to have people alongside you who are just wired like that and can't help themselves.

2. They know that being successful takes discipline, hard work and years of effort. In our 'quick fix' society, it's easy for young men and women to look with jealousy at people who seem successful, and overlook the blood, sweat and tears that have gone into getting them where they are. Christians especially need to remember that it's not just the people with a good heart who get the bumper hundred-fold harvest, but those who are willing to go and keep going.

3. They never settle and are always learning. When I meet very successful people, one of the things that challenges me is the amount of time they give to their own personal development. God can give us a brilliant piece of totally new thinking but so often he does that when we give ourselves to seeking, learning and developing. So much innovative thinking is now available to us literally at the touch of a button.

4. They deal well with failure. It's a fact of life that when you have a lot of new ideas, many of them don't work out. It's always OK

to fail as long as you learn from your experience, dust yourself down and get on with being entrepreneurial again. For the true entrepreneur, every challenge is an opportunity to grow.

5. They ooze faith and are fearless. If there is power in positive thinking, there is a whole lot more power in kingdom thinking, based on the Word of God. In his Word, God describes us as his masterpiece, designed to do good works which he has prepared for us to do (Ephesians 2:10).

Imagine what would happen if the whole body of Christ started to act fearlessly like these amazing entrepreneurs and step out in faith on whole new adventures for him!

# CHAPTER 10

# Remember the Power of Multiplication

## BEN JACK, ADVANCE

*True discipleship brings fruitfulness in evangelism*

I should start this chapter on multiplication with fair warning: as a teenager I had to re-sit my Maths GCSE exam *twice*. Truth be told, numbers have never been my strong suit, and yet as the head of Advance: The Message Evangelist Movement, I am now more concerned with multiplication than at any other time in my life. This isn't simply cold mathematics though – the multiplication I am talking about, when properly understood, becomes the most important pursuit of my life.

Through the Advance Evangelist Movement we seek to multiply and sharpen the number of preaching evangelists who will faithfully proclaim the gospel in and out of season, the goal of which is to see multiplication in the number of people worldwide who put their whole trust in Jesus Christ. So how can we ensure that we are facilitating and seizing upon opportunities for multiplication, and multiplication that lasts? How do we ensure our fruitfulness as evangelists, and see genuine growth in our churches?

Well, as limited as my mathematical ability may be, perhaps the basic principles of addition, division, subtraction and multiplication will serve us well as we consider how to see this fruitfulness and growth...

## THE LIMITS OF ADDITION

I often hear people reference multiplication in evangelism and mission strategy, when what they are really talking about is addition. The mentality can be, if I head out and tell one person about Jesus, then I've basically done my job. If that person receives Jesus as Lord, they can then go and tell someone else, and so on and so forth. One plus one, the gospel is spread and the world is (eventually) saved. However, there are two big problems with this approach.

The first is that addition-based evangelism becomes very functional and, dare I say it, somewhat legalistic. In other words, once I've gone and done my bit, I can sit back and rest easy with a clear conscience. The yearly mission trip to Africa? Check. The one-time offer to pray for a colleague? Check. The invitation to my brother-in-law for the Christmas carol service? Check. I'm not disparaging any of these things, but when doing them means we think we've covered our evangelistic bases for the foreseeable future, we really are missing the point of the gospel and our joyous role as messengers of it.

No one is more interested in multiplication than God. Upon creating the world, he tasks humanity to 'Be fruitful and multiply' (Genesis 1:28). In parallel with this, the famous final verses of Matthew's Gospel find Jesus 'commissioning' his followers to go into all the world and make disciples by the preaching of the gospel. Having populated the earth, we now needed saving from our rebellion against the King of life and love. Jesus' death and resurrection gave us the way by which this is achieved, and at the end of Matthew's Gospel Jesus tasks his followers with telling the world the good news that the kingdom is at hand.

This short passage has been more impactful on the instigation of church mission than any other. I've heard many sermons declaring the Great Commission as a command to be obeyed; going into the world to share the good news is something that followers of Jesus *must* do. I agree that evangelism is something we must do, but not because I think Jesus is commanding us to do it.

Whilst the word 'go' suggests a command element to Jesus' commission, it is surely of note that nowhere outside of the Gospels are Jesus' commissioning words quoted by the apostles. If this is a command to be obeyed, the apostles were not at pains to point this out to the early church, and yet the church flourished as the gospel was indeed lived and proclaimed.

Luke's account of the same events in Acts presents Jesus as saying 'But *you will* receive power when the Holy Spirit has come upon you, and *you will* be my witnesses in Jerusalem and in all Judea and Samaria, and to the end of the earth.' (Acts 1:8). Notice those affirmations of *you will*. Luke frames Jesus' words not as command but as promise, these things *will* happen. What we are talking about here is gospel identity; seeing the commissioning words of Christ not simply as a command to be obeyed, but as a promise and authorisation of the life that follows submission to his Lordship.

When I discover something I love, I share it with as many people as I can. Think for a moment about the last thing you passionately 'evangelised' about. A meal at a restaurant? A new TV show? A charitable cause? Did anyone need to tell you to do it, or did it just flow naturally from your experience? We don't share the gospel simply because we have been told to. We share the gospel because having received Jesus' transforming love for ourselves, we cannot stop talking about him.

So 'addition' models of evangelism are likely to view evangelism as a matter of duty, a task to be undertaken. But evangelism is a matter of identity, and you are never more human, never more your true self, than when you are declaring God's goodness to anyone who would listen.

The second problem of addition-based evangelism is that it underplays the power of the Spirit. If we want to see multiplication happen, we must plug into the source of power for the task. Hacking away at a tree with your chainsaw switched off is going to be a fairly fruitless exercise, more likely to damage the chainsaw than cut through the wood. Turn on the power however, and the outcome will be different. Whenever I share the gospel, to large crowds or one-on-one, I expect people to get saved (and they often do). Why – because I am a great evangelist? No, because God is a great God and he has authorised and empowered me for the task! This is what the Great Commission (in its various forms) tells me, and it matches up with my experience of stepping out in faith with this wonderful gospel that has lost none of its power to save.

One of our most ambitious projects is The Higher Tour, a huge outreach to young people across the UK that is, in part, inspired by findings within social science that suggest if just ten percent of a people group holds an unshakeable belief, that belief will be adopted by the majority. What should be of great interest to Jesus' followers is that these findings are based solely on societal trends, behaviours and influences, and yet they can yield powerful rates of multiplication. How much more can we expect multiplication to happen when the Holy Spirit gets involved! We should not be satisfied with the slow-turning wheels of simple addition in the church, but with uncontrollable yet authentic multiplication through the overflow of transformed Christian lives operating in the power of the Spirit.

## THE TRAGEDY OF DIVISION

Tragically though, the church has at times been better at division than multiplication. In 1983, Apple entered the Fortune 500 as one of the fastest-growing companies in US history. How did this relatively small technology company achieve such a feat? In short, Apple had a clarity of vision and led the market in developing and selling the most technologically advanced personal computers available, and invested in creative and high-profile marketing.

However, disunity and in-fighting led to co-founder Steve Jobs being forced out of the company in 1985 and by the late 80s, Apple was in trouble, losing market share to strong competition from the likes of Microsoft and failing to produce anything quite as innovative as those first revolutionary computers. It wasn't until the return of Steve Jobs and the announcement of the innovative iMac in 1997 that Apple began its journey to former glories and beyond, united once more by clarity of vision and innovation of product.

Disunity and division are never conducive to multiplication, so unity must be a priority, and for the church it must be unity in the gospel that we prioritise at all costs. Whatever secondary theological concerns we may have, whatever denominational differences and so on, we must stand united as one family bonded together through adoption by the saving work of the cross.

Apple's success could also be attributed to their marketing strategy during this renaissance period including the hiring of Guy Kawasaki as Apple's so-called company 'Evangelist'. Kawasaki says of his time at Apple, 'I learned that when people believe in your product, they will help you succeed through credible, continuous, and cost-effective proselytisation'.

Even in business, unity breeds evangelism! For Apple this looks like loyal customers buying and using Apple products, then singing the praises of these devices to anyone and everyone (again, not because they have been told to, but because they want to). How much more should this be the case for the church who have received true life through the gospel! For authentic multiplication to happen, we must keep the main thing the main thing: the gospel must be central to all that we are and do as individual believers and as the body of Christ. The reason many struggle to do this is because they are not sure what the main thing actually is, so…

## THE NECESSITY OF SUBTRACTION

It is time for us to get back to basics, to strip away some of the irrelevant noise and secondary practice and return to a deep understanding of the gospel itself. If we don't understand what the gospel is, how can we unite in its truth? To be able to live and share the gospel simply we must understand it deeply. This is not just an exercise in theological navel-gazing, but an attempt to understand what the good news really is, how it impacts our life, and how we share the message with the world.

One of the best things we can do in our church gatherings is to spend significant time reflecting upon the full truth of the gospel. It would enrich our worship, empower our witness, and glorify God. Subtraction is often viewed as a negative thing, but actually it can be very helpful to cut away, to prune for growth. Perhaps the time has come for the church to prune some of our excess away, and to focus in on that which is most important – the good news that changes everything, that makes our worship possible.

## THE POWER OF MULTIPLICATION

The goal of multiplication is not to create 'Christians', but disciples of Jesus Christ. 'Christians' as they are known today can go to church and never tell another person about the Bridegroom. 'Christians' can watch their favourite celebrity pastors preach up a storm on YouTube, yet never read the Word for themselves. 'Christians' can passionately sing the latest worship hit, but never spend devotional time in prayer with their Heavenly Father. Sadly, to be a 'Christian' doesn't necessarily mean an awful lot today.

But to be a disciple of Jesus Christ, well, that's something else entirely. A disciple, Jesus asserts, is known by their fruit. A disciple lays down their life in service of the King. A disciple is concerned only with Christ and him crucified. A disciple cannot stop talking about Jesus, even when faced with the most horrendous persecution or repercussion. A disciple is committed to living a holy, spiritually fruitful life that trusts in God's provision.

Although there is no silver-bullet, one-size-fits-all strategy that will guarantee multiplication, there is certainly one overriding principle: Disciples multiply disciples. The following discipleship keys have been essential in my own walk with Jesus, and are core principles of our Advance Evangelist Movement…

## 1. An unwavering commitment to prayer
We do not have the power to save anyone. In fact, God doesn't even need us to be involved, and at times works without or in spite of us! Yet he chooses and delights in making us part of his saving activity in the world. If salvation is a work of God alone, then the true power of evangelism is found in prayer.

## 2. A high view of scripture
One of the biggest obstacles to authentic multiplication in the church is biblical illiteracy. If we do not know what the Bible teaches, how on earth can we live out our faith with any integrity, and share God's truth with the world? We have a responsibility to maintain a high view of scripture, both in encouragement of personal, daily engagement, but also in standing united as a global church on the core tenets of the gospel.

## 3. Accountability

Honest and transparent relationships with trusted people in your life who can hold you to account for how you are living are essential. Holiness is our goal because it glorifies God, and a holy life will create curiosity and be attractive to those around you. A holy church will see authentic multiplication. You can't make someone else be accountable, but you can provide the framework through which they will have the best chance to be.

## 4. Sharing stories

The gospel is a story that is both fixed *and* ongoing. When we retell the fixed element of this story (the Jesus story – his life, ministry, death and resurrection) we are participating in the divine plan to bring humanity back to God by explaining the situation of creation, the fall, reconciliation and invitation. The ongoing story of the gospel is the way in which God continues to be at work in the world, and specifically our lives today (testimony). The ongoing story builds faith for the authenticity of the Jesus story, so let's tell both as often as we can, sharing the truth of what Christ has done, its implication for the world, and the reality of how it is playing out in our lives each day.

## 5. Asking for help

One of the terms we use at The Message to describe the journey we are on together is 'mates on a mission' – we are mates who help each other in the task. We must ask for help if we want to see multiplication happen. We ask God to help us by his saving, transforming power. And we ask each other, as one united family, for help in the task of seeing more brothers and sisters come home. Let's work together.

The best advice I have for you if you want to see multiplication in and through your ministry is to invest in your own walk with Jesus with everything you have, and encourage others to do likewise. And this is why multiplication becomes the most important pursuit of my life – because properly understood, it is a pursuit of authentic relationship with Jesus from which his truth will be revealed. Commit to being a disciple, and he will take care of the rest.

# CHAPTER 11

# Don't Separate Worship and Mission

## MEG LATHAM, WORSHIP LEADER

*Build a culture where worship leads to mission, and vice versa*

It was what I would call an interesting transition moving from my job as a nurse to come and work at The Message. I had got married, moved house and changed my career within the space of three weeks, and my head was spinning. My first week was a blur and apparently, according to the people in my office, I couldn't get out of the door quick enough when I had shut down my computer and finished for the day – I can laugh now! Going from a ward job to an administrative role as Carl Beech's PA sat behind a desk was quite the change and I was uncertain whether I had made the right choice.

I couldn't understand why and how I was in a nursing career one minute, and the next I was leaving it behind. Yet those initial few weeks felt like a breath of fresh air and as I worshipped and sought God, I felt peace. I knew I was in the right place at the right time, following God's will for my life.

As the weeks went by I started to get my head around what The Message was, and before long I felt part of the family. Sometimes life doesn't make sense and we get caught in a whirlwind of change moving us in directions we never imagined. We are led into adventures we never thought possible and, let's face it, those 'five-year plans' we make up are always prodded and shifted. Circumstances change, health changes, plans change. Only God remains constant.

So after a few short months of picking up the rhythms here at The Message I found myself leading worship and being released into what I can only describe as 'my calling.' Is that because I've found the one thing I'm going to do for the rest of my life? Is it because singing is 'my thing' and I love to do it? No, it's because I have found that worshipping every day is what I was made for. My soul yearns to worship. I long to be near God and he deserves my everything.

## DAY-TO-DAY AT THE MESSAGE

Every day looks different at Message HQ. On Monday, Thursday and Friday we dedicate the first half-hour of the day to devotion, prayer and sung worship. We extend this time on a Tuesday to a full hour, allowing further opportunity to worship together and to look at the Bible, inviting the Holy Spirit to speak to us. On Wednesday morning each department has its own team meeting – this looks different for each team, but we are all encouraged to pray together.

What a way to start the day! Prayer and worship are the foundation for everything we do at The Message and we make it a priority to start each day from a place of thanksgiving and praise.

Once a month we gather as a whole organisation for a day of prayer. This is an opportunity to hear updates and powerful testimonies from across the Message movement worldwide in an environment of worship. As we expand from a mission to a movement it becomes increasingly important to hear what each area of The Message is doing and to give space to focus on *why we do what we do and who we do it for*.

Prayer and sung worship isn't just limited to Prayer Days and morning prayers – throughout the year we have a number of different events where we corporately join to praise God. Vision Night is a good example – we gather together with our supporters to look back at what has been done over the past year and to celebrate God's provision. We cast the vision, seek new projects and dream big, but at the centre of it all, we worship and give him praise! Our worship is a catalyst for mission as we are filled up and sent out.

Our mission is all for Jesus. Our mission is to see transformed lives transforming lives. Our mission is to see hope brought to the hopeless. And we can't do it on our own.

The Message exists to proclaim the ultimate message: the message of the gospel, the good news. No matter what our background is, no matter what our story, Jesus came and he took on all of our mess, all of our brokenness and died on the cross so that we could have life. That is amazing news! There are beautiful stories of restoration and rescue bursting from every seam of The Message and no two stories are the same. We are all totally different from one another, with such diverse testimonies, yet we all stand side-by-side worshipping the same God who has saved us and is longing for the world to know him. That's the family we are a part of. Uniquely made and divinely intended.

## WORSHIP IS OUR PRIORITY

We are called to 'Sing to the Lord, praise his name, proclaim his salvation day after day' (Psalm 96:2). Scripture teaches us that worship can be outworked in our living, our speaking, our doing, and our adoration of God. At The Message we don't worship together just because it's nice to sing a few songs – we worship because we are called to worship!

Worshipping God when we feel 'on cloud nine' and everything's going well is easy but I think we please the Lord when we praise him in the tough times too, and make it a priority. The psalmist beautifully writes in Psalm 121:1-2:

> 'I lift up my eyes to the mountains—where does my help come from? My help comes from the Lord, the Maker of heaven and earth'.

When our souls are downcast and when we are struggling to see the good, lifting our eyes and worshipping despite tough situations and circumstances can transform our hearts and minds. As we worship we are reminded of who our help is, that he is the maker of heaven and earth and that he is present with us. Sometimes it's easy to worship, sometimes it's not, but we are called to it and we make it a priority here at The Message.

Worship isn't a response to how we feel, it is a response to the truth that has changed our lives and our outcomes. Feelings, emotions and negative thinking can hinder us – if we allow these to dictate whether we 'feel' God is good, or we 'feel' he is near, or we 'feel' like worshipping, we may have missed the point. Worship is a response to the God that made the stars and spoke life into existence, to a God who cares for the one, to a God that cares for you. Not only is it our calling to worship but when we grasp the reality of his gospel and what that means for us, it's an overflow of a life lived following Jesus. A reason we prioritise worship at The Message is to fix our eyes on him and refocus ourselves every day, no matter where we are at, because we aren't doing this mission alone. We do it with him and for him, and the more we know him, the more we reflect him.

## BRINGING WORSHIP INTO MISSION – AND MISSION INTO WORSHIP

I believe that being part of a missional movement requires us to first be on our knees and looking upward before we go out. We want everything to be rooted in prayer and filled with the Spirit.

As we pray and worship, we are revitalised and encouraged to go again in our mission. As we pray and worship, we stand in freedom to be repentant before our gracious Father and let go of anything which is holding us back. As we pray and worship, we have the opportunity to realign ourselves with the Holy Spirit and to seek the Father's heart. As we pray and worship, we are reminded of our identity in Christ, and surely that can only make us more effective in the work he sets our hand to.

We become game changers when we worship. As we spend time with Jesus we become more like him, and when we invite the Holy Spirit into situations we see spiritual temperatures rise and atmospheres shift. A back-and-forth attitude shapes our culture at The Message – as we springboard out of our worship into mission, we then return from mission with a worshipping heart, thankful for all God has done. Then we go again!

All our staff are encouraged with this and corporately there are lots of opportunities for us to engage in both worship and mission. I recognise that this is a privilege in my workplace but ultimately it doesn't matter what our context is, it's down to us to engage and recognise our calling to worship. He deserves our highest praise. So be encouraged that whatever your context and whatever your circumstances, worship him in all things and stand in the truth that you reflect the beauty of God.

# CHAPTER 12

# Remember You Are Salt, Yeast and Light

## SAM WARD, DIRECTOR OF MINISTRY

### IMITATING THE INIMITABLE

In Matthew's Gospel, Jesus labels his followers in two ways: as salt and light.

> 'You are the salt of the earth. But if the salt loses its saltiness, how can it be made salty again? It is no longer good for anything, except to be thrown out and trampled underfoot. You are the light of the world. A town built on a hill cannot be hidden. Neither do people light

a lamp and put it under a bowl. Instead they put it on its stand, and it gives light to everyone in the house. In the same way, let your light shine before others, that they may see your good deeds and glorify your Father in heaven' (Matthew 5:13-16).

We are salt, the salt of the earth. This phrase has become a popular term for someone who is gritty yet genuine, hard-working while a little rough around the edges. This was not Christ's intention for the verse, though. The description that Jesus gave to his followers was pointing to their purpose and their approach. To those who Jesus addressed on the Mount of Olives, salt had three clear uses: salt was a seasoning, a preservative and a disinfectant.

The imitators of the incarnation are similarly called to be high-impact people. Though small in number, they are to be added to community like a pinch of salt is added to a soup to enhance the *flavour*. We are those who 'move in and live deep' in our neighbourhoods. We are stirred in, invisible to the naked eye but irreversibly altering the very nature of our neighbourhoods forever. We are not just residents but we make our homes in places some fear to stay and others pass through.

Mission happens best when we live life fully. In John 10:10, Jesus expresses that he came to counteract the destructive work of the devil by giving us life, and life to the full. We are most missionally effective when we live in the fullness of the life Jesus has given us. Life cannot be put on hold for the sake of mission. The very purpose of our life is mission to the glory of God. We are given the flavour of the Saviour to make known the king and his kingdom. We are the condiment of the kingdom – we add life to a community. Our presence should bring blessing and encouragement. The people of God should celebrate well. We should be known as a party people. We open our homes and welcome others into our lives to 'taste and see that the Lord is good' (Psalm 34:8). We also empty our lives into a community in order to spice up the blandness of mere existence. The deeper we love, the more intense the flavour we add.

Though small in number, we are also to be worked into community like salt is worked into a joint of meat to *preserve* it. We are rubbed into our neighbourhood as a guardian, to uphold and sustain. We become woven into the fabric of our communities. We join school governing boards and residents' committees. We litter-pick the parks and mow the lawns of the elderly. We advocate for those who have no voice. We defend the rights of the broken and destitute. We prayer walk the street as though we were appointed to be 'watchmen on the walls' (Isaiah 62:6). We lock in the vitality of the neighbourhood, affirming what is good and pointing to what God is doing.

Though small in number, we are to be applied to our communities as a *disinfectant*. We pull down the structures and strongholds that stops people encountering and experiencing the one and only God, the strongholds that deny people from being with God: arguments that divert people away from God, imitations that distract people from God, lies that deceive people about him and falsehoods that distort the truth about him.

The greatest injustice in our neighbourhoods is not poverty, but the fact that poverty is keeping people from God. We are in a fight to reveal the character of God, a God who is rich in mercy, love and grace. A God who is forever faithful, who never leaves or forsakes, who is patient and slow to anger. A God who forgives sin and restores the broken. A God who is good and who joyfully delights over his people. A God who is peace. Where the enemy only seeks to kill, steal and destroy, we are the agents of life, revealing the giver of life. Salt is elemental: it cannot lose its potency but it can be diluted and we must guard against mission drift as we embed ourselves into community.

Though small in number we are also to be added to our communities as a yeast is added to dough. Tiny amounts of yeast have a great impact. We are the catalysts for transformation. We are called to be those who cause a community to rise and fulfil their potential, to be spread throughout the batch of dough triggering reactions. We are conversion agents, spiritually turning the lifeless starch into active sugar.

As a community rises, the transformation is visible to all. We have seen this first-hand in Openshaw. Our touchstone scripture was Isaiah 62 and from the start we prophesied these powerful verses over our community. Verse 2 reads, 'The nations will see your vindication, and all kings your glory; you will be called by a new name that the mouth of the LORD will bestow.' We saw this fulfilled beautifully on a number of occasions. After a few years of us living and serving, a billboard appeared on the main road that runs through to the city. The police had clearly paid for the advert which simply read – 'Crime in this neighbourhood has reduced by 60% in the last six months.' In 2006, the Independent newspaper ran an article titled 'The best place to live in Britain'. The article began, 'Renowned for its literary festival, its ladies' college and its majestic racecourse, Cheltenham has a new claim to fame – as the leading property hot spot in Britain. The Georgian town, situated in the heart of Gloucestershire and on the edge of the Cotswolds, heads a list of the nation's top 10 areas for property owners, published today. It is closely followed by Openshaw, in Greater Manchester.'

Second only to Cheltenham as the best place to live! Openshaw, Greater Manchester, a neighbourhood that at the time was the 11th most deprived neighbourhood in the England according to the Indices of Deprivation. The nations saw our vindication in the national press. We were no longer called 'Desolate' – our new name was 'Desirable and Longed After.'

## BEAUTIFULLY COMPATIBLE

The work of Eden is occasionally described as subversive. Like salt and yeast, we are invisible to the naked eye. We are stirred, kneaded and rubbed in. Yet Jesus wisely calls us also be light: a lamp on a stand, a city on a hill. We both are the 'salt of the earth' and the 'light of the world.' We cannot be hidden. The subversion to the salt and yeast must be held in tension with the light that cannot be concealed. Bright and brilliant, light contrasts darkness. Opposite and obvious, light dazzles in the night. Light is unmistakeably light, it cannot be disguised as anything else. Our message is distinct and undiminished. Salvation through Jesus Christ alone stands as a glaring beacon of hope for the world.

The Message Trust is known as a movement of evangelists. For 25 years we have been preaching Jesus. At every opportunity, no matter the occasion, we will call people to respond to the message of Jesus. It's in our name: we have a message and we exist to share it. The lampstand is the stage and street corner, the school and the bike shop. We cannot and will not keep silent about the saving power of Jesus. Christ is the way, the truth and the life, and we exist to make him known. We want our message to be blatant, to stand out and be seen.

Scripture tells us that 'God is light, and in him is no darkness at all' (1 John 1:5). Christ wonderfully describes himself as the 'light of the world' (John 8:12). Christ's death on the cross is the first and most glorious lamp on a stand. We have seen his great light and will relentlessly reveal him to others. We are his, we are children of the light. We are sent to continue the work of Jesus – we are now the light of the world. We have been transformed from darkness to light and that light can not be obscured. We want our words to be heard and not hidden. How can we hold back from declaring the great love God has for this people – how can we contain it?

Declaring the truth of Christ's death and resurrection for our salvation contrasts a culture where redemption is seen as an irrelevance. Love, faith and hope shine. We are called into dark places, never to become darkness or settle in the shadows, but to bring light. *The light shines in the darkness, and the darkness has not overcome it.* That's why we are unashamed in our reasons for relocating, and about the purpose of our presence. We are unapologetic in our proselytising. We are here to reveal Jesus.

So the call to be salt, yeast and light are in no way contradictory. They are beautifully compatible. We often make the mistake of associating 'salt and yeast' ministry as simply social action and 'light' as explicit gospel proclamation. But the effects of salt and yeast are meant to be visible! They are not simply good deeds done under the surface. They are transformational in nature and they are meant to point to the power of Christ. Hiding the knowledge of the saving work of Christ behind selfless acts of kindness is self-defeating. Social action provides us with incredible opportunities to explain the love of God. Likewise, a 'lamp on a stand' ministry is not simply preaching for a response. Christ exhorts us to 'let [our] light shine before others, that they may see [our] good deeds and glorify [our] Father in heaven.' This interweaving of word and deed ministry is intentional and it's incredibly powerful. Our good works must shine the light of Christ. Our identity as light-bearers must enable people to taste and see that God is good.

I love this twin track approach of The Message Trust: courageous incarnation alongside bold gospel proclamation. We will never be purely a social action movement. We have the greatest news to proclaim, and this news should always be accompanied by good works. In fact, it is as we hold these two elements in tension that we best reveal the kingdom of God and bring it near. Our ministry of reconciliation works best as we first reconcile word and deed in our witness.

CHAPTER 13

# Take Responsibility

## IAN ROWBOTTOM, OPERATIONS DIRECTOR

*Lead by assuming the best, avoiding the void, and planning well*

As The Message's Director of Operations, I'm usually landed with the jobs no one else wants to do! A big part of my role is keeping the wheels turning: turning our bold vision into reality and keeping it there. Like many leaders, I was thrown in at the deep end and have had to pick up a lot of leadership and management skills along the way. In this chapter, I'll share some of the key lessons I've learnt to help prevent you from making some of the same mistakes I have. Each relates to an understanding that how we act as leaders affects those we lead, either for good or ill. If we learn to lead well, we not only advance our work but also train the next generation of leaders in the process.

It's always encouraging to read a great leadership book and find that one of the key principles is something that you've already happened to pick up along the way. This was the case when I started reading *Extreme Ownership* by Jocko Willink and Leif Babin. The premise of their book is that, as leaders, we have to take ownership of absolutely everything in our sphere of influence. This can be hard because our natural tendency is often to blame others for problems – but when we step up and take responsibility, it can be incredibly liberating.

A number of years ago, when The Message was a bit smaller, we would celebrate everyone's birthday across the whole organisation. This meant that every few days you would be asked to sign a pile of birthday cards. One afternoon I was signing a whole bunch of cards with my usual 'Happy Birthday, have a great day, Ian', when I realised that I had just signed it on someone's leaving card. Fortunately, at the time there was another Ian in the organisation – Ian Henderson – so like any good abdicator of responsibility, I added an H to the end of my name. In his book, Jocko Willink says: 'Leaders must own everything in their world. There is no one else to blame.' Turns out, Jocko, there is! You just need to have someone in the organisation who shares your name.

The first principle of taking responsibility is making sure that our pride doesn't get in the way of admitting mistakes, even if others ought to share the blame. A few months ago, I was part of the team organising our biggest fundraising event of the year. On the night, there were a number of issues with the venue and, in particular, the schedule the catering staff were working to was wrong. It didn't come to light until 15 minutes before we needed 800 meals served that they were going to be bringing the starters out half an hour late. I quickly checked the running order we had sent them and, sure enough, we had told them the correct time – but somewhere along the way there had been a mistake. It would have been really easy to panic and start blaming the venue, but in that moment, it wouldn't have helped at all. What we needed to do was work together to get the food out as soon as possible so we could get the schedule back on track.

Once we'd got things sorted, I started thinking through how frustrated I was – but I quickly realised that earlier that day, I had spoken to the catering staff but hadn't been proactive in double-checking that the details were correct. Yes, I could blame the venue or some of our junior staff, but the bottom line was that I was the most senior person on-site all day and it was ultimately my responsibility to make sure that everything across the board was running smoothly.

When we take responsibility as leaders, it helps those we lead to feel safe. They know that we're not going to bite their head off for something which has not gone to plan; more importantly it focuses us on fixing the problem rather than getting into a blame game. When I spoke to one of our staff who was also organising the event I started with, 'This was my fault. I should have checked.' Immediately, I could see the relief on their face and this meant that they could get on with organising the rest of the event without the fear that they were going to get into trouble. I had to put my pride aside in order to take responsibility. It's so easy for pride to get in the way, but as leaders we need to make sure that this never happens.

There are other benefits to this way of operating. It helps build trust within a team and demonstrates that it's OK if we fail. There's nothing better for giving a team the permission to try new things and be creative without the fear that if things don't work out, they are going to end up in trouble.

## DEALING GRACIOUSLY WITH OTHERS: ASSUME THE BEST

A number of years ago I managed a guy who was totally sold out for the mission of the organisation and worked really hard. However, there was something about him that seemed to cause him to struggle. I felt like his primary school teacher might have said, 'He doesn't play well with others.' His attitude was exemplary, but he just found it hard to get things done and was often in conflict with those who worked with him. It took me a really long time to realise what the issue was. When I did, I saw how destructive his behaviour was for those around him and how much of a negative impact it was having on his outlook on life. I realised that he really struggled to assume the best of others. This might seem like a really small thing, but it can be massive. Always choosing to assume the best intentions of others allows you to view people and situations in a much more positive way.

We should always give people the benefit of the doubt and assume the best intentions. I wonder whether the reason this can often be hard is that many of us have been taught that we shouldn't assume anything when it comes to our work. Maybe you've heard the phrase that if you assume anything, particularly in the context of project planning and working with others, and your assumption then turns out to be wrong, 'it can make an ASS out of U and ME.' When it comes to people's motives, though, we should think differently.

What I would see happen time and time again with this guy was that when he would get an email from a colleague which presented some sort of problem or issue, he would immediately jump to the conclusion that either the sender was trying to make his life more difficult or that they were simply incompetent. He found it really hard to understand where others might be coming from, or that they might be facing challenges he knew nothing about. We have to be people who give others the benefit of the doubt and assume that they have the best intentions. In most cases, they usually do!

If you encounter a situation where someone has made a decision that you are not happy with, it's always worth bearing in mind that the other party is probably trying to do what they believe is best given their position and experience. It's extremely unlikely that you're going to come across people in ministry who are trying to sabotage your work. So, before you moan about them behind their back or confront them to their face, consider why they might have made their decision. If you think you have new information which might lead to a different outcome, be gracious. In my experience, it's often the case that the other person has more information than you, and that the right decision has already been made.

Acting in this way will not just improve your relationships with others and ensure a much more pleasant environment to work in, it will also have a huge impact on your mental health when you don't jump to second-guess everyone else's intentions.

## SOLUTION-DRIVEN PROBLEM SOLVING: AVOID THE VOID

I will always remember a partners' meeting I attended at my church soon after I joined it eight years ago. My church leader was leading the session and he said something that has always stuck with me. He said, 'As church partners, I don't want you to come to me with problems without also bringing a way of fixing them as well.'

I think one of my natural gifts is to see where problems are and how we have arrived at them. I'm also quite a good problem solver, but the reason what he said stuck with me was that I noticed that I would often go into meetings and explain a challenge without any real thought as to how we might go about fixing things. I think it was because, at the time, I didn't have a huge amount of leadership experience and naturally wanted to defer to others in the team. In reality, I had been given responsibility for an area and what I really needed to do was to step up and lead alongside those I'd been put with. Not to do so was actually unfair to the rest of the team.

But this isn't quite the whole picture. What I've discovered about our leadership team is that, as a group of external processors and activists, when a problem is presented our immediate reaction is to try and fix it. Usually this works brilliantly and we quickly land on a great solution. Sometimes though, we can arrive at a solution that doesn't really work. The sense of pressure to fix problems, even when we don't have all the relevant information in front of us, means that we can make a poor decision which in turn needs to be fixed later on. Problems always need solutions, but it only works if those solutions are good.

I call my principle to address this 'Avoid the void.' When there is a void of good ideas, the vacuum that is left can be filled with just any idea – and it's often a bad one. When presenting a solution alongside a problem, it can be based on hard facts and proper thought. That way, it's much more likely to be successful. It sounds blindingly obvious but you'd be surprised how often this can completely shift an outcome! Most of the time, these solutions end up being an amalgamation of an initial well-thought-through idea and the wisdom of all those in the room. I think the key to this is to never start with a blank piece of paper.

## PROPER PLANNING: PREVENTING POOR PERFORMANCE

A few years ago, when we first started looking at expanding The Message internationally, we asked a leader from another Christian organisation to come and speak to the team about his experience of doing the same thing. He was a huge blessing to us and gave us loads of great advice, but one thing he said really made me think. He talked about their mantra, 'We get ready on the way', meaning when they felt it was right to start a new project they just went for it and figured out how to do it as they went along. We could easily identify with this – The Message is an organisation that has always been quick to move when we've felt led into new areas, and often we've had to 'get ready on the way.' On many occasions this has served us well, but as we grow and the complexity of what we do increases, we have to be careful that we don't use this as an excuse not to prepare or plan well. If we're not careful, 'getting ready on the way' can look like someone who got up late and is trying to get out of the house with a wonky shirt and their trousers around their ankles!

Here are five keys to good planning that I find give the maximum chance of success for any project or mission...

**Work out your big picture goal: what are you trying to achieve?**
This might sound really obvious, but it's all too easy to plough ahead without thinking this through. Then, things start to go adrift because the goal hasn't been clearly defined. It's vital to allow time for strategic thinking. Initially, this might be on your own but it's always good to involve others. Do whatever it takes to allow time for big-picture thinking – including taking your team off-site if you get too distracted in your workplace. It's also really important that the rest of your leadership team is on board and has clarity about what you want to achieve.

**Create a strategic plan.**
One of the questions Andy asks constantly is: 'Has anyone done a critical path?' It's a great question! What he means is, 'Do we have a plan of how we get from where we are now to where we want to be? What are our specific goals, timings and milestones?' There are plenty of great tools available to help us do this. However, this alone isn't any good unless you also communicate your plan to all those involved – until then, it's nothing more than a thought in your head.

**Pull together a team.**
I've come to recognise that my natural tendency is to try and do things by myself. But in my experience diversity leads to better

strategy. Having people from different backgrounds, disciplines or ages can bring a real strength to a team as each member draws on different experiences to work together towards a common goal. A diverse team is also the perfect environment for helping more junior staff to learn new skills – and comes with the bonus of helping to share the workload in the process.

**You have to shout 'Action!'**
It doesn't matter how good the plan is if there are no specific actions attached to it. Implementation is the phase that turns strategies and plans into actions, in order to accomplish what you have set out to achieve. Actions assigned to people move a strategic plan from a document that sits on the shelf into real change. The plan must clearly articulate goals, action steps, responsibilities, and specific deadlines. One thing to really watch out for is to make sure that before closing the planning session it's clearly explained what comes next and who's responsible for what.

**Don't write it in stone.**
Good plans are fluid, not rigid. They should allow you to adapt to changes within the structure and goals you have set together. And don't be afraid to scrap plans altogether if necessary! Don't waste time and energy on something that's not working and never will. If pride is the only thing that's keeping you going, it's the wrong motive.

A team of people who take responsibility in a radical way will always be more successful than one where everyone plays the blame game. By always assuming the best, dealing in the currency of well-thought-through solutions, and planning well, you'll notice a step-change in how successful you can be when it comes to keeping the wheels of an organisation turning.

# CHAPTER 14

# It's All About Passion

## ANDY HAWTHORNE, FOUNDER AND CEO

*Of all the things we hold dear, passion is most important*

The British supermarket chain Sainsbury's recently launched a campaign with the strapline 'It's our values that make us different.' At The Message, we know that's true of us, too. An organisation like ours is shaped by its vision, but it's driven forward by its values. We have four values that we try to live by, and which, we believe, make us who we are.

Anyone coming for interview as a staff member or a key volunteer receives a CD with four talks from me explaining what our four values are, and why they're so important to us. We basically say, 'Listen to this, and if you don't agree with them then probably don't come for interview! But if you do, we think you'll love it here, so come to your interview expecting to be grilled on them!'

Church is one of our key values. We are deeply rooted in local church, and I love the fact that on our staff we have members of churches from pretty much every stream and denomination. Part of our regular line management is asking people how committed and accountable they are to their local church, because it really matters.

There have been times where I have felt intensely frustrated by the church – maybe you can relate! Sometimes our Sunday gatherings can seem very inward-looking, and our mission very safe. But I'll never forget one time in the home of a couple of our supporters, on my knees, pouring out to the Lord a complaint about the church. At that moment, I sensed God gently rebuking me in my spirit, 'Don't you dare diss my bride! You may think she's got zits and halitosis. But she's beautiful and I love her. And if you love me, you're going to love her.'

That's why in every place we work, we make it clear that we are there to serve the local church: we will always do things together with the church and we never plan to set up our own denomination. It doesn't matter if The Message gets the credit – if the church wins, we win. We believe the local church has the hope of the world – the life-changing, good news of Jesus – and our job is to encourage and guide the church to get that hope to the places where it's really needed.

Community is another key value. Jesus chose to work out his ministry with a bunch of friends, saying in John 15: 'I no longer call you servants, because a servant does not know his master's business. Instead, I have called you friends, for everything that I learned from my Father I have made known to you' (v. 15). The one true God lives in community as Father, Son and Holy Spirit and we work out our friendship with him not only vertically, but horizontally – in community with one another.

You've already read in this book that we like to think of ourselves as being 'mates on a mission.' It's interesting to track the ministries that have really made a mark for Jesus over the generations, because they tend to be a bunch of friends who journey together through thick and thin over many decades.

In the post-war era the ministry that won more people for Jesus anywhere in the world was the Billy Graham Evangelistic Association. But although it was Billy's name on the signs, the truth was, this incredible mission was accomplished by Billy Graham *and his mates* – a group of young American guys in their sharp suits who travelled with Billy wherever he went and were deeply committed to the same mission. There was Cliff Barrows – probably a better speaker than Billy himself – leading the sung worship. There was George Beverly Shea, a revered gospel singer who came along to perform each time Billy got up to speak. There was T.W. Wilson, working in the background, sorting out all the logistics.

When Billy did the last ever mission, guess who the worship leader was? Guess who got up to sing before Billy spoke? Guess who was in the background, making the whole thing work? Right through their lives, they stuck together as a community. And look at the fruit. They went around the world lighting gospel fires for well over half a decade. Cliff Barrows said of the group, 'Life is not a solo existence. Effective work in evangelism is not a solo ministry. It is a team of people whose hearts God has knit together.' How about that? The way to really make a difference is to get God's vision for your life, get some friends to join you on the journey and stick it out through thick and thin, for the long haul.

Another of our key values is innovation. As you've read in Chapter 8, for us it all started with our touchstone scripture, Isaiah 43:19 – 'See, I'm doing a new thing…' God spoke it to Isaiah hundreds of years before Christ, God spoke it to me in 1987, and God speaks it to all of us today, too. The Message is an organisation all about the 'new thing', believing that God has many good works up his sleeves, planned for us to do. As a movement we have been given the gift of innovation – the ability to come up with world-changing sparks of innovation. Not every idea is a good one, but lots of them are. When we land on one which works, we go after it. And there are so many more ideas to come.

I'm writing this in 2017, and all around the world people are marking the 500th anniversary of the Reformation. Back then, innovators like Martin Luther and Thomas Cranmer dragged the church out of the rut it had got stuck in, back into renewal and life. From a place where the church was locked up in hierarchy and the religious spirit, and scripture was inaccessible to ordinary people, the reformers set people free. Their motto was *semper reformanda*, 'always reforming' – holding on to ancient gospel truth but conveying it in the language and culture of the present day. We're about the same business.

In 1896, the Director of the US Patents Office is believed to have requested that the organisation be closed down, '…because everything that's going to be invented has surely been invented by now.' Sometimes, unwittingly we can get into this mindset, too. But

God is always about a 'new thing.' We need to be praying all the time, 'God give us a new thing! A new sound. Something to grip people, to wake people up.'

I'm determined to build a culture of ducking and diving, constantly trying new things to make Jesus known and to bless his world. I'm determined not to be a bottleneck of vision and want to make trying new things as easy as possible. Of course, the truth is, that as long as you are genuinely rooted in local church, and you're in high-quality, accountable relationships in a healthy community, anything goes. You are almost always going to hit on some great new innovative stuff to change the world in Jesus' name.

However, number one among our four values, the one which in many ways undergirds all the rest, is passion. First and foremost, we are a passionate people. Passionate for Jesus, passionate for the poor and the broken, and passionate to reach those who don't know Jesus as their Lord and Saviour. Wherever I go, people say to me 'Wow, you're a passionate guy aren't you?' and I tend to think 'Am I? I'm just me!' But if I really am passionate about the most important things, then I call that high praise because it is only the passionate people who ever change the world.

I know I'm actually pretty average. Average height, average weight, average intelligence, one wife, two kids, living in a semi-detached house – all pretty boring stuff apart from one exceptional thing, a passion that I discovered when I decided to follow Jesus. There is a quote we love at The Message that goes like this: 'Where work, commitment and pleasure meet, you reach that deep well called passion. Here, nothing is impossible.' I long for The Message to be a bunch of people who embody that, not clocking on and clocking off, but giving our all with exceptional passion.

In Romans 12, Paul commands us to 'never be lacking in zeal' and to 'keep our spiritual fervour' (v. 11). This suggests to me that we can lose it, and that zeal and spiritual fervour is something that we need to keep stoking through intimate encounters with Jesus, experienced through prayer, passion and worship, digging into the Bible and by stepping out in faith. I know I'm biased but I honestly believe there is no better place to stoke that kind of passion than The Message.

One of our early songs has the line, 'All over Manchester I wanna see revival!' In that shout is where this thing started, and where it will end. We are a revival movement. God's promised us that we are going to see rivers in the desert... we'll see wild animals honour him because that's what they were formed for... we're going to inherit a land for Jesus.

In the early days of The Message, I know we were a bit extreme and in some ways acted like crazy people, working ridiculous hours and giving above and beyond to reach those who don't know Jesus. We were driven by utter passion. Maybe it was over the top at times. Maybe we did work too hard. But I never want to lose that zeal. As my friend George Verwer puts it, 'It's easier to cool down a furnace than warm up a corpse.' Wouldn't it be great if we found ourselves visiting churches and Christian conferences and having to say, 'Will you lot just calm down a bit? You really are getting a bit overexcited, passionate and radical in your attempts to reach a lost and hurting world!'

It's hard for me to write about passion without referring to General William Booth again. After his death, his son Bramwell said this of him: 'The thing that impressed me most about my father was that the sins and miseries of his fellow men had scorched him like a flame'. I love that the fuel that led his incredible revival movement that blessed the poor like perhaps no other street movement in the history of the church was one man's extraordinary passion. He saw prisons emptied, communities transformed and hundreds of thousands swept into the kingdom of God at a time when the world population was about 10% of what it is today. God, give us more young men and women marked out by that kind of passion, who embark on their own passion-fuelled rescue missions!

Passion makes sure you don't do 'a reverse Jim Collins', and go from 'Great' to merely 'Good'. Many amazing revival organisations throughout history have lost their zeal and their spiritual fervour over time. I could name loads of organisations which are still doing good work, no doubt, but they're not the revival movements they were when they started. In each case, what goes missing is the passion of the early days – the unshakeable belief that they have been called to make a difference in this world, whatever the personal cost.

To conclude, when it all comes down to it, I guess what we're really looking for is more people who are authentic followers of Jesus – the One who, wherever he went, displayed extraordinary levels of passion. Whether it was weeping at his friend's funeral or looking at the crowds and his heart breaking for them, wanting to gather them up like a mother hen gathers her chicks.... Whether it was getting zealous for his Father's house and casting out the money changers who had turned what was meant to be a beautiful relationship with God into some religious money-making exchange that ripped off the poor, or being moved with compassion whenever confronted with the poor, lost and broken... Jesus was Mr Passion and if we are to have any chance of changing this world for the better, we need to do all we can to stir up our passion towards the things that really count.

Because Jesus inspired Paul to write those words, 'Never be lacking in zeal', we know it can happen. Every command of scripture can be turned into a promise. It means that all of us really can have spiritual fervour, all of the time. We may display it in different ways, but we can all be passionate people. So take responsibility, examine yourself. Stand before Jesus and ask yourself if you've lost any passion. And if so, get it back.

# Thanks for reading

So there you go – you've had a little insight into some of the things God has helped us discover on the quarter-century journey from a one-man band to the global movement we are becoming today.

We are not for a moment pretending to be the biggest or the best ministry. We just know that God has raised this thing up and continues to bless it in the most ridiculous ways. If we can help others to have their own adventures with, and for, Jesus, then maybe the stream we are seeing in the desert could become a river, and then a full-blown flood. Bring it on!

## Wondering if BEING THE MESSAGE might be what you were made for?

### LIVE

We have teams across the UK, South Africa, Canada and increasingly around the world. And we're growing all the time.

. . . . . . . . . . . . . . . . . . . . . . . . . . . . . . . . . . . . . . . . . . . . . . . . . . . . . .

Read about our work and get in touch at **message.org.uk**

### TRAIN

Message Academy is ten months of intense training in the dynamic, faith-filled atmosphere of Message HQ in Manchester. It's designed to help you discover your place in God's mission.

. . . . . . . . . . . . . . . . . . . . . . . . . . . . . . . . . . . . . . . . . . . . . . . . . . . . . . .

Find out more and apply at **message.org.uk/academy**

### GIVE

Become a regular supporter and stand with us to see lives changed by the good news of Jesus. Hear the big news first through our regular Flow magazine and Prayer Calendar.

. . . . . . . . . . . . . . . . . . . . . . . . . . . . . . . . . . . . . . . . . . . . . . . . . . . . . . .

Get connected at **message.org.uk/give**